UNINTENTIONAL
Music

For Sylvia

Thanks so much for
helping us to connect
with our baby! Kai

LANE ARYE

UNINTENTIONAL

Music

Releasing Your
Deepest Creativity

HAMPTON ROADS
PUBLISHING COMPANY, INC.

Cover design by Marjoram Productions
Trumpet images © Nick Rowe/PhotoDisc
Miscellaneous cover images © Steve Cole/PhotoDisc

John Cage excerpt from page 8 from *Silence*
© 1973 by John Cage, Wesleyan University Press,
by permission of University Press of New England
Haiku from page 17 of *On Love and Barley: Haiku of Basho*, translated
by Lucien Stryk (Penguin Classics, 1985), copyright Lucien Stryk, 1985.
Reproduced by permission of Penguin Books, Ltd.
Submitted excerpts from *Tao Te Ching by Lao Tzu,
a New English Version,* with foreword and notes by Stephen Mitchell.
Translation copyright © 1988 by Stephen Mitchell.
Reprinted by permission of HarperCollins Publishers, Inc.

Hampton Roads Publishing Company, Inc.
1125 Stoney Ridge Road
Charlottesville, VA 22902

434-296-2772
fax: 434-296-5096
e-mail: hrpc@hrpub.com
www.hrpub.com

If you are unable to order this book from your local
bookseller, you may order directly from the publisher.
Call 1-800-766-8009, toll-free.
Library of Congress Catalog Card Number: 2001094080
ISBN 1-57174-260-3
10 9 8 7 6 5 4 3 2 1
Printed on acid-free paper in the United States

For Markus Marty

One need not fear about the future of music. But this fearlessness only follows if, at the parting of the ways, where it is realized that sounds occur whether intended or not, one turns in the direction of those he does not intend. This turning is psychological and seems at first to be a giving up of everything that belongs to humanity— for a musician, the giving up of music. This psychological turning leads to the world of nature, where, gradually or suddenly, one sees that humanity and nature, not separate, are in this world together; that nothing was lost when everything was given away. In fact, everything is gained.

John Cage, *Silence*, 1961

Table Of Contents

Acknowledgments

Deepest thanks to Arny Mindell who developed process work and changed my life. This book is an extension of his ground-breaking work. It was he who suggested that I explore the unintentional aspects of music, and he who encouraged me to write this book. He is a constant source of inspiration and love.

Special thanks to Christoph Heer, a true friend and co-researcher. His willingness to experiment and his motivation to learn and grow gave me a unique opportunity to cook my ideas and methods in a friendly pot.

Loving thanks to my mother, Leonora Arye, for teaching me about the unintentional at an early age, for infusing me with creative spirit, for encouraging me to tell her awesome story, and for her friendship; and to my father, Leonard Arye, for his unending support and love in spite of all my youthful *mishugas;* and to my brothers, Lowell Arye and Larry Arye, for being behind me every step of the way.

Many thanks to Dawn Menken for introducing me to process work and suggesting that I move to Zurich to study it; to Joe Goodbread, who encouraged me to hold onto my passion for music while studying psychology, and who helped me immeasurably with the subchannel concept; to Renata Ackermann, who was helpful, supportive, insightful and amazingly generous with her time during the first version of this work; to Markus Marty for his keen eye, hard work, warm heart, and spirit; to Richard Leviton and Frank DeMarco at Hampton Roads for believing in this project and making wonderful suggestions which improved the book; to Michael Peus for experimenting with me at the beginning of my quest to combine music and process work; to Marvin Surkin for his support during the first version; to Wendy Davis for sharing her research on creativity; to Clare Hill for many fascinating discussions about speech, sound, and precise description; to Jan Anderson for introducing me to a community of inspiring people who stammer; to Julie Diamond, Alison Lee, and Greg Rodehau for help with intention; to Cynthia Mitchell for supporting the artist in me and allowing me to reproduce portions of her play here; to Tomasz Schwed for his authenticity; to Margie Simpson for her generosity; to Sharon AvRutick for her friendship and her amazing editorial talents; to Amy Mindell, Arlene Audergon, Rhea, Sara Halprin, Selina Gan, Jane Kepner, Justyna Kaczmarek, Judith Jones, Diane Butler, Matt Guynn, Andrea Battermann, Helmut Eisel, Nisha Zenoff, Magdalena Schatzmann, Flo Mizelle, John Booth Mizelle, Ursula Hohler, Franz Hohler, and Karen Elias for helpful feedback; to Margaret Ryan for her heartfelt and masterful editing; to Lecia King for her excitement and her fresh perspective; to Veronica Vass for support and insight at a crucial moment of writer's block; to Judith DivaBear Jones for turning me on to "Somebody's Knocking" and supporting this white boy's love of gospel music; to Bobby McFerrin for teaching me that freedom includes discipline and learning; to Aretha Franklin for singing from the depths of her soul; to my friends in the process work community who live double lives as musicians, artists, poets, and dancers; and especially to all the musicians, writers, artists, students, and clients who opened themselves, showed themselves, transformed themselves, played great music, and taught me to sing again.

Preface

I always loved singing more than anything else. I loved the release, the joy, and the passion of self-expression. Even in the midst of the worst despair, singing would save me. I sang everywhere—in stores, on the street, in buses and trains. People often smiled and commented on my good mood. That surprised me, since I was not always in a good mood. I was just singing. They did not differentiate the excitement from the pain, the loneliness from the love. No matter what I was expressing, they heard happiness. And, in a way, they were right. Because those holy sounds transformed everything inside of me into ecstasy. I loved nothing more than this, and wanted to devote my life to it. I studied voice, guitar, music theory, jazz theory, and improvisation. I sang in bands, and played in clubs and festivals.

But something horrible happened. The more I learned to sing *correctly*, the less contact I had with why I was singing in the first place. It felt like there was nothing inside me to express anymore, or I didn't know how to get in touch with it. Instead of paying attention to the music we were making together, I wondered if the other musicians liked my singing. On stage, I heard myself through the audience's ears instead of my own. Thinking it was all due to my lack of talent and experience, I practiced harder. It only got worse. I knew all the grammar but could not form a sentence. I had nothing to say. I felt empty. Then I met Arny Mindell, the man who developed "process work."

Arny reintroduced me to myself. His way of looking at the world and at people opened my eyes and my heart. His special quality of love, his openness to the irrational, his unending spirit of discovery and delight, changed my life. Process work is a tool for awareness and personal development. More importantly, it is a trust that even the most disturbing experiences can, if followed, lead us in the direction of change, growth, connection, and wholeness. I think of it as riding the hidden wind. Process work helped me to get in touch with something essential, authentic, and meaningful. I moved to Zurich, Switzerland, to study it full time. Eventually, I became a process worker and started to help other people find the magic in their lives.

For years I rarely played, rarely sang. It simply gave me no joy. Whenever I did, I couldn't stop imagining an audience and how they would react. I was always one step removed from the experience. But I was still passionate about music. I listened voraciously to the blues, gospel, old soul music, old R&B, jazz, and rock. And I started to research ways to combine music and process work. While we were running together one afternoon in 1988, Arny suggested that I focus on *the music that people do not intend to make*. This casual comment became the focus of my creative and intellectual life.

I started to give seminars about unintentional music. Usually lasting a weekend and taking place in various cities around the world, these seminars are places to explore the irrational and unexpected things that happen when we play music. The participants range from musicians, music teachers, and music students to people with no musical experience at all. Often people attend who are sure they cannot play or sing, or who have been traumatized by criticism of their early musical attempts. In addition, there are usually psychotherapists, as well as people who are just interested in voice, music, or sound, or who want to learn about themselves.

Participants sit in a circle while one person at a time comes into the middle with me. There, she plays music, sings, talks, or makes any kind of noise. The two of us then notice and "unfold" the music or sound she was not intending to make. As you will see, working with such "mistakes" can have transformative effects on both the music and the musician. Seminars are also geared toward training the participants to work with their own, and other people's, unintentional music.

Over the years, I have given many private sessions to musicians, singers, conductors, and the like. These sessions are very similar to unintentional music seminars, except that they take place between only two people. I have occasionally taught voice and guitar lessons, encouraging the students' "mistakes" when more conventional methods had fallen short. After working with musicians for years, I started to give seminars on creativity, exploring what happens *unintentionally* in all kinds of art forms.

During much of this time, I saw myself as someone who helped other people with their music and creativity. I loved the contact, the newness and wonder that occurred every time I worked with someone, the intense curiosity about what could possibly arise from some unwanted sound. But sometimes I was jealous of the musicians in my seminars. Deep inside, I longed to be making my own music. Then one day something wonderful happened. I noticed myself humming. A quiet, ordinary hum—but it came from inside and filled my body with delight. I focused on that sound with the same loving attention that Arny had focused on me, the same loving attention that I had learned to focus on the musicians with whom I work. It no longer mattered whether I sounded good. Curiosity had replaced judgment. Wonder had replaced technique.

I started to sing whatever sounds I heard inside or outside of me. It was fun, funny, moving. I discovered sounds I did not know my voice could make. I let my body teach me. I began to luxuriate in the feeling of my fingers as they sank into the fretboard of my guitar. And now the smallest seed of melody or harmony, the subtlest hint of a feeling or thought, when focused on with that slow, intimate caress of awareness, grows into a song.

Once again, my deepest loves and hates and follies and pains and joys are channeled through music. I no longer do "normal" vocal exercises, yet my voice is stronger than it used to be, with a bigger range. I don't think about what hip note to sing but, somehow, ones I like pop into my ears and out of my mouth. Most of all, I feel that what I am singing is true. Whether a gentle whisper or passionate cry, my own composition or an old favorite, the music rises from somewhere deep inside. Even when I sing in public, I am often able to hold on to that vital core. Process work helped me to get back in touch with myself when I sing. Or maybe it helped me to get out of the way.

A note on language:

Unintentional music happens when people sing or play any instrument (or just make sounds). In order to make the text easier to read, I have opted to write "play," even when I mean "play or sing or make sound." I likewise use "musician," even when I mean "anyone at all," which fits with my conviction that everyone is a potential musician. And in the interest of simplicity (as well as to balance thousands of years of "he"), I use the pronoun "she" rather than "he or she."

A note on accuracy:

The examples in this book come from more than thirteen years of work with musicians, artists, and others in seminars, classes, music lessons, and private sessions. These stories have been related to the best of my ability, often with the help of videotape and copious notes. Wherever possible, I have checked with the people described here in order to make sure that my accounts accurately portray their experiences.

Part I

Playing The Music
Of Your Dreams

Don't come to us without bringing music.
We celebrate with drum and flute,
with wine not made from grapes,
in a place you cannot imagine.

–Rumi

Introduction

Strange, discordant sounds came unwanted from my guitar. It was supposed to be a love song. Yet each time I sang a certain verse, my fingers played the wrong notes. I started again, enjoying the harmony of the chords, singing the soft melody, until I came to the same passage and my fingers again refused to play what I had composed. How puzzling. The sound was so weird, so different from the feeling of the rest of the song. I tried once more, this time making the mistake on purpose. My eyes slowly moistened as I realized that this particular line described what life had been like before meeting my beloved. The out-of-tune notes evoked that same longing and emptiness. I decided to include the "mistake," feeling that the moments of dissonance made the song more poignant.

Whenever we create, just like in other areas of our lives, some things happen that do not go along with our intentions. The unintentional aspects of the music we make—the unwanted note, the cracked voice, the strange croaking sound we try to avoid, the rhythmic problem we cannot erase even after hours of practice—contain more wisdom than we think. The same is true for the unexpected splash of color on the canvas, the ungraceful turn on the dance floor, or the writer's block that makes us pull out our hair. They are intimations of parts of ourselves, and of our music and

3

art, that lie beyond our awareness. Exploring the unintentional with curiosity and love can help us to tap into the wellsprings of our deepest creativity, and make our music, our art, and ultimately our lives, more authentic, meaningful, and original.

But how can we believe in things we don't like? Why make music that sounds wrong? Shouldn't we focus on improving the things we are trying to do and make every effort to make our art the way we want it to be? What could possibly be useful about troublesome interferences?

There is an old Jewish story about a king who had a large diamond that was exceptionally pure. He was very proud of this peerless gem. One day, though, there was an accident and it was deeply scratched. All of the diamond cutters agreed that the imperfection could not be removed no matter how much the stone was polished. But one artist engraved a delicate rosebud around the imperfection, using the deep scratch as the stem of the rose. The diamond became even more beautiful than it had been before the accident.

An old Taoist tale tells of a man who meditated in the mountains. After a few years, an immortal appeared and asked the man what he was doing. He replied, "I am trying to meditate on that mountain, but there is too much fog for me to see it." The immortal laughed and disappeared. The man went back to his meditation. A few years later the immortal returned and asked the same question. The man replied, "I am meditating on the fog." At this, the immortal bowed low and said, "You are my teacher."

These stories illustrate ancient truths. Rather than ignore or try to get rid of the things we don't like, we can transform them into things of beauty, or shift our focus and realize that they are what we have been seeking all along. Like the alchemists who sought to transform base metal into gold, we too can be enriched by the things we normally consider to be garbage.

This perennial wisdom is at the core of *process work* (or process oriented psychology), a strange and wonderful way of perceiving and interacting with people and the world, that was developed by Arnold Mindell. Whatever happens unintentionally—what disturbs you or ruins your best plans—can, if followed, turn into a thing of great value and meaning. When something unexpected or disturbing happens, this signals the appearance of Nature, of the Tao, of Spirit, of God. Every culture has its own name for it.

Mindell calls it the *dreaming process*. The process worker's job and passion is to find, support, and unfold the dreaming process in all areas of human experience. Originally developed as a form of psychotherapy, process work is now applied to such far-flung spheres as dreams, physical illness, extreme and altered states of consciousness, comatose states, dying and near-death experiences, meditation, relationships, group dynamics, organizational development, and conflict resolution.

This book shows how to follow your dreaming process as you are actually making music. These methods work equally well with the voice, any instrument, and any style of (written or improvised) music, with professional musicians and people who can't carry a tune. You'll see that the same ideas and tools can be used with all kinds of creativity and expression. Such work can be incredibly fun and exciting. It also produces unexpected and powerful effects on both the musician/artist and the music/art itself. The line between self-discovery and creativity blurs as we cross between these two seemingly separate realms and find that they actually complement and enhance each other. The door between these worlds is the unintentional.

I once worked at a seminar with a professional flutist, Sharon, who began by playing a beautiful, meditative, Japanese piece. I was entranced by the loveliness of the music and her full, smooth tone. But I noticed, at times, a breathiness that seemed unintentional. Sharon said that she had often been disturbed by this breathiness, which she could not get rid of, despite years of practice and work on her technique. I asked her to intentionally play even more breathily. When she did, there was more vibrato in her playing, the sound now making the air in the room undulate. As this next unintentional signal was encouraged and Sharon tried to play with more vibrato, she complained that she had to use lots of air. I suggested she use even more air. But then she could only play short phrases, because she ran out of air too quickly. When she did this on purpose, the way she held her mouth got sloppy, and so the tone became very weak.

A few minutes before, Sharon had played beautifully. Now, after following a succession of unintentional signals, she could hardly play at all. At such moments, I tend to wonder whether anything useful can come out of all of this, and sometimes I start to feel sorry for the unfortunate person who volunteered to explore her unintentional music. But then I remember how many times such processes have been transformed, how many roses have grown out of irreparable scratches. I relaxed and continued.

I asked Sharon to allow her mouth to get even sloppier. When she tried to play this way, no tone came out of the flute at all. I thought, there you've done it, Lane, you have ruined her playing. But I waited. She said, "I have no voice." Then she started to cry and said, "I never had a voice." She told me that no one has ever heard her in her life, that she feels powerless and defenseless. I asked her to play that feeling. A barely audible, sorrowful melody came out of her. A few seminar participants began to cry. Suddenly, in the middle of a note, she stopped. She said a voice in her head had told her to stop. She realized that this voice is the one who always stops her. This is why she has no voice. This is why no one hears her—because she is never allowed to express herself.

Blood surged to Sharon's cheeks and her eyes opened wide as the effect of this inner voice became clearer to her. She was furious that it had stopped her all her life. I suggested that she pick up her flute again and first play the voiceless one, then the stopper, and finally her reaction to the stopper. This was incredible. At first she played with lots of feeling and almost no tone, the same mournful tune as before. Then came a loud sudden note, followed by silence. Then she began to play frenzied, wild, violent, angry, ecstatic torrents of notes. It was passionate and intricate, resonant and complex. It came out of her like a volcano erupting, like a machine gun, like an ecstatic dance, like the spit that was flying from her lips.

When she stopped, she just stood there for a long time in awe of what she had done. She had never played like that before. She had had no idea that it was possible to play like that. She did not even know all of those emotions were inside of her, much less that she could express them with her flute. She did not know this part of herself or of her music.

Was this music or was it self-discovery? Yes. Unintentional music led Sharon inside herself to places she had never known. And it helped her to play music in ways she had never imagined. Music and personal growth are intertwining lines of a dreaming song.

Music is my passion and the focal point of this book. But everything discussed here can be applied to any creative medium. Actually, you can read the whole book thinking of music as a metaphor for whatever you want to create, or however you want to express yourself. It's shorthand. Every time I write "unintentional music," feel free to read unintentional painting or writing or film or dance or whatever your chosen medium is. You can use these same principles all the time, whether speaking in public, talking with friends, making love, planting a garden, decorating your home, or whenever you feel inspired or seek inspiration. Life itself can be your creative project.

This book is meant for musicians and people who are convinced they will never be musical. It is for artists of all kinds and people who think they don't have a creative bone in their bodies.

It is for anyone who longs to express herself more fully and authentically. For that person who has always been told how boring and average she is, whose tiny creative spark just needs a little love and encouragement to turn into a creative flame. For that person who was stopped at an early age from trying new things, who dreams of the courage to experiment. For anyone who has experienced blocked creativity and is looking for ways to tap back into the source of inspiration. For anyone who wants to walk the path of heart, and yearns to open her ears to an inner guide. For music teachers and music students, art teachers and art students. For music therapists, art therapists, speech therapists, and psychotherapists. The many examples I've included will give you a taste of the huge variety of ways that unintentional music arises and unfolds. I hope that by reading about other people's experiences, you will be inspired to explore your own unintentional music.

A strong wind is blowing outside my window. I can't see the wind itself. But I can see the leaves shaking on the trees, the sheets billowing like sails on the clothesline. In the same way, the dreaming process—though impossible to see directly—affects you and your music in untold ways. If you tap into that mysterious source and learn to follow it, you and your music will never be the same.

Chapter 1

Zen Blues:
A Taste of One Man's Unintentional Music

A good artist lets his intuition
lead him wherever it wants.

–Lao Tsu

There was a winter chill in the air, though it was only October. Forty-five people sat close together on chairs and pillows at the Process Work Center in Warsaw, Poland. It was one of a series of classes on unintentional music. Someone turned on a video camera. As I looked around the room, I saw both old friends and new faces.

Tomasz (pronounced Tomash) was there for the first time. I liked him the moment I saw him. A fit, boyishly handsome man in his late forties, he had smiling eyes. He felt gentle to me, warm, unassuming. So I was a bit surprised when he spoke. I had asked for a volunteer to say something so the others could describe what they heard. Tomasz spoke in a loud, theatrical voice, making everyone laugh. That staginess did not fit my initial impression of him at all.

What I didn't know was that I may have been the only one in the room who had no idea who Tomasz was. Something of a star in the Polish country music scene, he had recorded many records of his own songs, been on TV many times, and was the founder and organizer of an annual country music festival that had become a Polish tradition. Looking back, I'm glad I didn't know any of that. Because when it came time for me to work with someone, Tomasz raised his hand. I'd like to think that I would not have been distracted by his fame, that I would have treated him like any other person. But I'm not sure. I may have tried to impress him, or to impress the class with my ability to work with him. Maybe not, but I'm glad I didn't have to find out. For me, Tomasz was just another friendly face in the crowd.

The mood was playful as we moved to the center of the room. Although Tomasz spoke mostly Polish (and I, mostly English, with a translator between us), he jokingly peppered his speech with American phrases like, "yeah, man" and "cool, baby." I was enjoying the game and thickened my New York accent. I asked whether he played music. He said he was a singer and played guitar. "Alright," I said, "me, too. What kind of music?" He replied, "If I had to name it, I'd call it folk. My own music. I started playing a little country . . ." The room broke out in laughter. I didn't see what was funny, which made them laugh more.

Tomasz took out his "harp" (blues harmonica). I asked him to play something, saying that it did not really matter what he played, since I was listening for what he did not intend to play. He wiped his lip, scratched his nose, cupped both hands around the harp, put it to his lips, and blew tentatively. A few notes sounded, softly, just for a second. After a moment of silence, he played a single note a bit louder, held it and bent it. Then, much louder, he played an up-tempo blues, bending lots of notes, and tapping his foot to the beat. I know it's ethnocentric, but it always surprises me how well Polish musicians can play the blues. The musicians in my band in Warsaw really had a feel for it. So did Tomasz. I had to stop myself from singing along. When he finished, the class applauded.

In an exaggerated American accent, Tomasz said, "Yeah. You know what I mean, man. Tough life, ain't it?"

I was curious about this continued joking. It was like Tomasz was playing a role, not being himself. I didn't know what to make of it and wanted to keep the focus on the music, so I went on.

I had been most interested in the first, quiet chord—the one Tomasz had played before he really started playing. The rest of what he played had sounded intentional to me; but that soft, short blow was totally different. Tomasz smiled and nodded. "When someone expects you to say something, at the beginning it is ... " He took a quick breath and held it. "I said the first word," he went on. "I heard how it sounded. Then I knew." I mentioned that that first, quiet sound he played was very different from the loud and theatrical sound of the first words he had said in class. Tomasz replied, "Yes, I knew then what I would say before I began. When I was playing, though, I was not certain at first. Later, I knew what I wanted to say." I invited him to experiment with the kind of sound that had happened before he knew what he wanted to say.

Tomasz played a soft chord. Then silence. Then a soft note. He said it was soft because he was uncertain. I encouraged him to explore that soft, uncertain sound. He played a few more notes, then hit a "wrong" note. It was the first time he played a note out-side the blues scale he had been using. This made him stop and look at me. I encouraged him to go on with more "wrong" notes. He started to make weird sounds with his harp on every in-breath, each time slowly exhaling without playing. This breathing created a structure. He was using the exhale as a way to keep a slow beat and to frame each experimental sound. He stayed within this form until, at the end of one phrase, he accidentally exhaled into the harmonica. Out popped a few notes that had no melody and broke the rhythm he had established. Tomasz made a face. "It was so nice until then," he said. "I didn't want that sound. It was not sup-posed to be there."

I said I was interested in the sounds he does not like. He replied, "They're too simple. It can't be that way." Why not? "It's plebeian." Putting his hand over his mouth as if he understood something, he said, "It must be art. Real art. I have to feel it is real, true. It should connect with my emotions. That other sound was schoolish." He wrinkled his nose. "Like a child who takes a violin in his hands for the first time. Accidental. It's an accident. It doesn't fit any structure."

I had already noticed Tomasz's inclination to stay within a structure. His blues fit a form. The soft notes fit into a scale and the phrases had a beginning, a middle, and an end. Even when I had recommended experimenting with the "wrong" notes, he had done so in a structured way.

"That's right," I said. "You like structure. And that's good. But you are also interested in art. Truth, actually. And I wonder whether there could be something true in that accidental thing, something that is not included in your structure. Maybe truth is coming from another part of you that you are not in touch with yet."

"Yes," he said. "I know that's right and I don't want it. Because it is a worse side of me."

I didn't know exactly what he meant, but went on. "You think it is a worse side of you. But since you're interested in truth, why not let that 'worse' side play? Just for five minutes. You can always go back to playing the 'nice' part."

Tomasz took a deep breath. He hesitantly put the harp to his lips, put his hands down, raised the harp again, lowered it and said "Blah!" He smiled, tried again and stopped again. I asked what was happening. He said, "It is necessary to blow." He took a deep breath, cleared his throat, inhaled, puffed out his cheeks as if he would blow and said, "It shouldn't be great, right?" "No," I said. "It shouldn't be. That's the point."

Tomasz immediately put the harp to his lips and blew one quick chord. Then he played the first line of "Oh Suzanna" in a very simple way. Then played some random notes. Some low, some high.

12

I asked him which of all that was the "worst." He said, "The fact that I don't control it. I am not the master. It irritates me because those are not my things." I wondered aloud whose things they were then. I asked him to play like that again and, at the same time, imagine someone who would play that way. He knew already. He said that a child, about five years old, would play like that. What it was like to be five? Tomasz said it had been painful for him. I gently asked whether it would be okay to say a bit about what was painful? He said, "Those are things I have put in order somehow. Accepted. I can speak about them easily."

I said, "You have an incredible way of putting things in order. It is a beautiful thing about you." Tomasz looked touched, like I had seen him. I went on. "Your ability to put things in order is an important quality in your personality, and in your music, too. I imagine that the five-year-old did not have that ability yet."

"He had sensitivity," Tomasz said. "I feel a potential, a creative potential there. I am limited to constructing things. It is difficult for me to release a real creativity."

"That is the point we're at right now," I said. "You have a way of constructing forms that are ordered. But, like you're saying, you get blocked in that moment when you could get out of those forms and into really creating something." Tomasz nodded in agreement. "And in that moment," I continued, "those unintended sounds that you hate could be helpful. The ones that break your form. That five-year-old has a lot of creative potential."

"Yes," Tomasz said excitedly. "Because, you know, he hears sounds in a different way. He gets to know them for the first time. In a fresh way. Yes . . ." Tomasz took a deep breath. "You touched. You touched something."

"So maybe you can let him play something."

Tomasz looked distressed. He scratched his head, then shook it. "No," he said. "I'm not prepared to do that yet."

"Yet," I said. "That means you will be able to do it later?"

"Yes. I'm getting closer to it. I know I'm in a process. I'm getting closer."

"I'm not going to force you to do anything," I assured him.

"I'm afraid," he said. "I'm afraid to release emotions that are very deep. I would despair. Well, I am not sure if fury is stronger or despair."

"That sentence," I observed, "is the adult trying to order whether the feeling is fury or despair. The five-year-old just has emotions and does not wonder what they are. He just has them and expresses them."

"But, you know," Tomasz said, "when you let out emotions at that age, things are not so smooth."

I could have asked what had happened when he had let out emotions as a child, but I decided on a different route. "I hear you backing off, so I am not going to push you into anything," I repeated. "But I'd like to ask you something else. You said you are not ready yet. That means that later you might be. I wonder what will be different later."

"It would be the same."

"Then why later?"

"If I would be in this group for some time. If I knew people ..." Tomasz looked down at a woman sitting on the floor. They both smiled. He kneeled down with his arms open and asked, "May I?" She responded warmly and they hugged. "You looked at me so nicely," he told her.

"How did she look at you?" I ask.

"Warm. I got support."

"That touches you."

"Women have supported me my whole life." He looked pensive, then continued. "But I don't want that now. If she supports me, I will run away from myself and into her."

"Does that mean," I guessed, "that your wish to have the group's support is also not good for you? That you need to do it anyway, with the support or not?"

Tomasz paused for a long time, put a hand on the back of his neck and smiled. "Yes," he said slowly. "I just don't know what is real. First I produce a sound and later a sound pulls me. I don't know when I am true."

"You don't know me," I started. "You never met me before. You have no reason to trust me. But in my experience, the things that happen beyond our intentions when we play are real. In the moment, those unintended sounds are outside of your form. But they are coming from somewhere. I'm guessing that they are trying to teach you a new form. You don't have to do it now. You don't have to do it at all. Or you can do it when you are alone at home. Or you can do it now. It is up to you. I just want to put that little seed inside of you."

Before I could even finish my sentence, Tomasz blew a note. Then another. I said, "OK, you decided to do it now. Go for it."

He played a very soft note. Then a loud bent note. Then more, getting louder, faster. It sounded expressive, explosive, angry. Then he kneeled down on the floor. I asked what had happened. He said he felt weak.

I said, "OK. You played something that was not weak. Then you felt weak. So now play something that is weak."

Tomasz started to play very softly. The notes were breaking up. It sounded imploring, aching. Like a baby crying, moaning. It got louder again and faster. Then softer again and slower. I don't have words to describe the music he played. It was blues, but not in any form I had ever heard. I just know it went right through me and made me shiver. Tomasz stopped. He wiped his eyes and nose of tears and snot.

"Real," he whispered.

In His Own Words

Tomasz's work really touched me. More than that, Tomasz himself moved me. I was impressed by his courage, by his ability to go deep, and especially by his realness. What may not have come across in the description was the authenticity of what he did. Sure, at the start of the work he was fooling around. He seemed to be putting on some kind of act. But soon afterwards it became very real. He never jumped into something just because I suggested it. At each moment he questioned whether what he was doing was right for him, whether it was true in that moment. Even when he was saying that he did not want to let the "worse" side of him play, that was real. In fact, it would not have been authentic if he had just done it, against his better judgment or against his will. He went step by step, staying close to his feelings. And when he finally did decide to let that other side of him play, he totally let go and went with whatever happened. Not only could you hear the difference, you could feel it in the air.

That authenticity made me want to have more contact with him. We arranged to meet and jam. We had a great time sipping scotch, singing old songs, and listening to each other's originals. By then my friends had told me who he was. This piqued my curiosity about whether our work together had any impact on his music making. About a month after the session, we met again and talked about just that. Here is a sample of the things he said that evening. If some of the language sounds a bit awkward, it's because we were speaking a combination of English and Polish, with no translator.

I asked Tomasz about his general impressions of the work.

"I was trembling at first because of the group. Someone recognized me. I felt I had to be good to confirm my status. I was frightened. It was like an exam. I felt I had to show people what I know, what I can do. You helped me. I saw you were friendly and open to me. I could be playful with you. At the start, it was kind of a game, but then I gave up the game and started to work seriously with the sound.

"I blew and the sounds appeared. I heard it but didn't control it. It was very irritating. It had to be good. It had to have a melody. It sounded childish. I felt I had to show you the highest possibilities of my art. But you let me play this way. You let me play my inside. I know I started crying with the harmonica.

"Before, when I was playing the blues, it was only a type of song. Blues. But when I was playing at the end, it was sadder, more tearful. I found more feelings inside of it. I remember the taste of it. Because it was mine. Not an African American sitting on a dock in Louisiana somewhere. It was mine. My sadness. My blues.

"There is a kind of border. I sometimes balance on it. On one side there is me: educated musician, singer, composer, lyricist. The commercial me. On the other side—sometimes I am on the other side—the real creation, the real truth happens on the other side. It's not that I'm lying when I am commercial. But that first side is craftsmanship. On the other side—where the truth is, where the real feelings are—there is a kind of creation. It's like Zen archery. Shooting happens by itself. It shoots itself. It is the same with that kind of creation. It appears. It appears without my conscious thinking. That's what I'm looking for. I have only had a few moments like that in my life. But that is what happened in our work together. It played itself.

"After our session, I remembered the strange emptiness of it. And I knew that when I would try to do it again, I would have to call back that emptiness. How to describe it? I was clear. Something like I forgot about the scale, about harmony. I forgot my musical knowledge. My criticism. There was only sound."

I asked Tomasz what had helped him to get to that point.

"You told me with your body, with your eyes, with a smile, that nothing bad will happen. That you accept everything. You told me, 'Show me everything you want to. It doesn't matter what will be because everything will be good and proper. Everything that you will do is important and has its own value.' That was a kind of message. I remember your eyes. I remember my embarrassment when I played that wrong note. I looked at you in a quick glimpse. Then I looked in your eyes, but very deeply. I think I was trying to check if you were serious, if I can trust you. You were waiting for me with kindness. That was the first step for me. You told me, 'everything you do will be good.' Unconditional acceptance. As a result of that, I was able to give that acceptance to myself. I am used to something else. When I am good, they treat me right. When I am bad . . . you know. But you told me, 'There is no old rule now. Be yourself. I accept this.' That was a relief."

I asked whether his music had changed since our work. At first he wasn't sure. He had not given it much thought.

"I'm not sure it happened in that very moment, but in my last concerts during the last month, I feel more calm. Something made me more sure of myself. Oh, I can build self-assurance artificially. For a long time I behaved like that. But now I feel it is truer. I had a TV concert two weeks ago. In the past, in such situations, always I felt very nervous and was thinking what would happen and how it would be. This time I just made the program for the concert, went there and played. That was all. I felt very calm. I'm not sure it is a result of our work, but maybe yes.

"I also started to be more brave in concert. There have been a few moments in concert where I started to break the forms. Using my voice in a different way. I started to interpret the songs more. I caught a few moments that fly out of the structure. They are still within the composition but I treat them more easily. Not conventionally. It goes without my consciousness. I let myself be more elastic. An unintentional ornament. I sing the old song, but with fresh notes. Maybe only a couple of times in a song, but it is fresh. I let myself do something out of the rules that I used before. I gave myself the right to treat notes more freely. I like it."

What about his compositions, I wondered. Had he written any songs in the past month?

"Yes, of course! I wrote two songs I really like. You touched something there. I didn't realize it started to work. It is like a clock hanging on the wall with the pendulum standing still. You moved it. You told me, 'Why not play with sounds?' I said, 'I can't play stupid tones. I have to play the right tones.' You told me, 'Why don't you treat music like fun, playing with the tones?' So I started to play squeaky, strange sounds and tones. I hated them at the beginning. I am a serious musician. I have no time for stupid tones. Later, I found it interesting. I think that was very important for me. It was a kind of possibility.

"Maybe that is why the last two songs I wrote appeared as a result of playing, as a result of fun. For the first one, I used an Indian harmonium, a squeezebox. It makes a solid background with one chord. Because there are only two tones—the fifth and the tonic—you can use any scale. I sat down with this text I had written and started to play the squeezebox. It went so easily. I sang it from beginning to end, the first time. Usually I treat composing rather seriously. I build something, make it. But this was so natural, obvious, evident. I didn't put up borders or limits. I didn't think about forms. There were no rules. Only fun. And I really like the song.

"In the other song, I used my guitar in a different way than I used to. I always use triads, chords with three tones, and make a structure with a basis of three or four chords. This time I used chords with only two tones, the tonic and the fifth, repeated in octaves. It's simple. I use the same fingering but in different positions on the neck of the guitar, with very small variations. It amazed me that I can do it in this way. Because I moved beyond my own structure in composition. It's like I changed the rules. It's not that I planned this. No. It's just how it played. It played itself. Usually I try different ways to work with a text or music. But this time, like with the squeezebox song, it just wrote itself. I felt it happened outside my consciousness. That was a special kind of fun."

I asked whether this kind of fun was similar to his playfulness at the beginning of our work.

"The fun that happened in my songs is different from the funny one at the start of class. That was a funny person made by me. That was not a real one. It was the clown. I know my clown. He is made for the other people. To make them laugh and make them treat me right. It's for sale. These two songs, though, are not cheating. I know that they are the truth. I, myself, had fun writing them. It was not that I made someone else have fun. I didn't think of others. I was glad to sing them, to play with the notes, with the words. I know that when I'll sing the squeezebox song, everyone will be laughing and it will be fun for them, too. But more important for me is that it was fun for *me*.

"There are two ways of creating: touched by Apollo or touched by Dionysus. Dionysus is this one I am talking about. With fun. Without thinking about it. Without heavy, hard work. Just like this," Tomasz said, snapping his fingers.

Identities, Edges, and Getting Out of the Box

Tomasz identified himself as being a professional musician—which meant, for him, playing well, being an artist. It was important for him to know what he wanted to say with his music before saying it. There is nothing wrong with that. In fact, I wish more musicians would care about what they are saying instead of just producing a bunch of notes. But sounds that did not go along with Tomasz's identity showed that the dreaming process was stirring his soup.

Those uncertain, out-of-tune, out-of-control tones were so irritating to him. "Plebeian," "schoolish," and "childish" were words he used to judge and put down the strange sounds. Tomasz would much rather have controlled everything and kept the music within a known structure. I was excited, though, about these "mistakes" that did not fit into any form, especially when I heard how adamantly he dismissed them. His strong reaction was a good indication that something important was hiding in that "childishness."

One of the striking aspects of the session with Tomasz was that the work seemed to stall a few times. He stopped and would not, or could not, go on. For instance, he did not want to let what he called the "worse side" of himself play. He raised and lowered his harmonica a few times, smiled, tried to start, stopped again, made strange faces and sounds. In process work we would call this *being on an edge.* An edge is the limit of your identity; it is the limit of what you can do, the limit of what you know. On one hand, Tomasz did not want to play because he did not like that "worse side" of himself. But, he also *could not* do it, because he did not have the slightest idea of what kind of music that other part of him would play. It was so far away from anything he knew, that he must have felt like he was staring out into a vast nothingness. Tomasz's strange behavior was more than understandable—even typical— given the circumstances.

Tomasz eventually did play something, which he said was music like a child would play. Then he came to the next edge. Although he said that the five-year-old held the key to the real cre- ativity that Tomasz longed for, he would not let that kid play. At such moments, it is important to be gentle but firm. Be gentle in the sense that you should not push yourself (or another person) over the edge. Don't force yourself to do something that is not right for you in the moment. Edges are useful and should be treated with respect. Without them, we would not know who we are. But edges also limit our wholeness by cutting off parts of ourselves that do not go along with our sometimes narrow identities. So be firm in your awareness. Don't forget that you are on an edge. Stay there and discover everything you can about it. Because that edge is the place of growth, both musically and personally.

I met a visual/performance artist today who knows nothing about process work. When I told her about this book she said,

"Mistakes are where the exciting things happen in art. But there's a certain amount of bravery involved. They take you to places in your soul where you don't always want to go." Tomasz was standing at the gate to one of those places. When he summoned his bravery and stepped in, though, he found it was not as terrible as he had feared.

That evening in class, the five-year-old taught Tomasz how to play with deep feeling. Possibly more important for Tomasz's work as a musician, though, the child got him out of his box, out of his structure. That boy knows how to listen in a different way, to hear sounds as if for the first time; he has what Zen Buddhists might call a beginner's mind about music. It is not surprising, then, that Tomasz compared the experience to Zen archery and recalled the emptiness, the clearness, the music playing itself. This state, this quality of listening, breathed new life into Tomasz's music. The blues were different than he had ever played them. His old songs became elastic and fresh. He found new ways to play his guitar, to write songs. What Tomasz had thought of as childish and unworthy of his talent turned out to be a divine child with a whole new approach to music.

How can it be that after feeling and expressing such deep emotions in class, Tomasz played with such fun and ease at home and in concert? Do those experiences have anything to do with each other? Remember that Tomasz identified himself as an educated and serious musician. He worked hard at crafting and building his compositions. Letting a melody play itself, letting a song write itself, went against his normal way of seeing himself and making music. I asked Tomasz about this. He told me, "When you are a child, parents give short sentences that lie inside you for a long time. For me, it was, 'Nothing comes easily.'"

In essence, Tomasz was hypnotized by this sentence at an early age, and it became rigidified into a belief system that kept him locked into his "normal" way of thinking, playing, and composing. Such belief systems lie at the foundations of our edges, keeping the walls intact, keeping us in our place. If "nothing comes easily" and everything good comes from hard work, then it makes sense that Tomasz would look down on melodies that appeared effortlessly, like gifts from the wine god.

Luckily, the five-year-old remembered those magical times before that unfortunate sentence existed. When Tomasz thought about being small, he remembered the pain, the anger. But perhaps there was another part of that child as well—the original joy, the unbridled playfulness, the time when everything came easily. No, it was not surprising that Tomasz could now write fun-filled songs. But thinking that fun was the point of his process would trap us in yet another box.

Remember that Tomasz did not know what would come out if he let the child play. "I am not sure if fury is stronger or despair." He was trying to name the experience in advance, in the same way that he liked being certain of what he wanted to say before he played. Later, though, something different happened. Music came out fast and furious, until weakness made him sink to his knees. When he followed the weakness, he played the tearfulness inside him. Tomasz had become a Taoist, able to move fluidly from one emotion to the next and back again. It could have been fury or despair or joy or humor. He got out of the way and let it play itself, whatever "it" was. This is why the music was real, not a product of his thinking or an artful interpretation of a preexisting construct. It was a fluid expression of his moment-to-moment experience.

"I remember the taste of it. Because it was mine."

Try This:

1. Pick up your instrument and test it before starting to play. Or hum a note just to test your voice before starting to sing.

2. Notice the quality of this music that happens before the "real" music begins.

3. Try playing something, anything, with this same quality.

4. Is this different from the way you normally make music?

Note: You can do this same exercise with any medium. For instance, pick up your brush, charcoal, pen, or pencil and test it before you begin to paint or draw. Or test your balance or your weight on the floor or make random movements before you start to dance. Or test your computer or your pen by writing random words before really starting to write. Continue the exercise in your chosen medium.

Chapter 2

Riding the Hidden Wind:
Process Work

The breathiness coming from Sharon's flute, that first, soft chord from Tomasz's harmonica, were secrets waiting to be told. They were the white crests of waves, barely hinting at the depth and power that were driving them to the shore. To the musicians, they were disturbing or, at least, insignificant. But when given attention and permission, the processes implicit within those mundane signals began to show themselves, like buds opening into flowers in spring.

In order to help such buds to bloom, and to understand the rest of this book, it will be useful to know something about process work.

Taoism

Process work is deeply rooted in Taoism. Unfortunately, the Tao itself is impossible to define. Lao Tsu, the ancient Chinese sage who is considered to be the father of Taoism, wrote in his immortal classic, the *Tao Te Ching,* "The Tao that can be told is not the eternal Tao." So anything I say will be inadequate. Still, the Tao is so central to process work that I must try to describe it, knowing I will fail.

I think of the Tao as an unseen wind, a current that moves the 10,000 things along its path. What the Taoists call the 10,000 things—all the things we can perceive and experience—are always changing, and those changes go in a certain direction. That direction is what we call the Tao. It can be thought of as the order of Nature. It is not God, in the traditional sense of a ruler or architect who wills things to be. Rather, it is the dynamic order that structures the way things are.

The ideal of the Taoist is to be in harmony with the Tao, to move in the direction that it moves. In Chinese, this is called *wu wei*, which literally means "no action" or "not doing." But the Taoists are not suggesting we do nothing. Rather, wu wei means not doing anything that goes against the Tao. In other words, it is beneficial to do things if they go along with or further Nature.

Let that cursory and insufficient description suffice for the moment. We will return again and again to Taoism, and you will hopefully get more of a feeling for its beauty and wisdom. By the end of the book, it should be clear that process work with unintentional music is actually applied Taoism.

Interlude: Snail Music

Most of us would like our plans to be fulfilled, our wishes granted, our prayers answered, our hopes and expectations met.

But things don't always work out that way.

So we fight and scream and kick and scheme and rebel against fate and do everything in our power to alter the course of history in our favor.

Which is great. When it works.

Sometimes, though, we find that no matter how hard we try, the world is how it is.

Abandoning the struggle, we float downstream. The river carries us without effort.

As the piano teacher chided his student to play faster and faster, and the girl took all the time in the world to study the keyboard before striking the first chord, the Tao poked out its laughing head. "This time, play the piece faster!" the teacher cried. And the student, with infinite patience, positioned her fingers over the keys, decided they were not quite right, and began the whole process anew.

The teacher finally realized the foolishness of trying to ride a snail like a stallion. Encouraging the girl to play as slowly as she could, he relaxed and listened with amazement to the depth of emotion and presence that was expressed in the simple melody, a tune he had heard hundreds of times in hundreds of lessons, but never like this. Transfixed by the power of the Tao, he was speechless.

C.G. Jung

Process work also stems from the work of C.G. Jung, who was interested in not only the cause of a problem but also its purpose, its final goal, the direction it is leading us in. Jung's perspective differs from the causal thinking that is most clearly represented by Western medicine. When a person gets sick, the doctor looks for what caused the symptom to occur. Then she gets rid of the cause, if she can, thinking that the symptom should disappear as well. Someone thinking about purpose and final goals, on the other hand, would see the symptom as a signpost pointing toward potential growth and development. Her challenge would be to discover in which direction the symptom is pulling the person. Like the Taoist, the finalistic thinker does not try to change Nature but, rather, to follow it. She believes the things that happen are meaningful events.

Process work sees even disturbing or unwanted things as potentially meaningful. This, too, has its roots in Jungian psychology. Jung believed that dreams often compensate for a one-sided conscious attitude. To give an example from my own life, I spent much of my childhood and early adult life feeling small and weak and victimized by people whom I experienced as being bigger and more powerful. I often dreamed that huge men were running after me trying to catch me. These dreams made me feel even smaller and more terrified. I interpreted them as confirmations that I really was the miserable little thing I always thought I was.

According to Jung's theory, though, these men represented a side of me that was far from my normal way of thinking about myself. They were a compensation for my one-sided attitude about the world and myself. When I started process work and saw those dream figures as my *teachers*, my life began to change. I slowly discovered my own power and stopped feeling like a victim. As my attitude changed, my dreams did as well.

One night I dreamed, as usual, that huge men were chasing me. Each of them was as big as a house. This time, though, I stopped running, turned around, and asked them what they wanted. They told me very politely that the professor had sent them to teach me about being a man. I dropped down on my knees and said, "Please teach me." They proceeded to show me how to find precious stones and roots of trees inside of a huge mountain. They showed me the softness of a rose and how to twist its stem in order to avoid the sharpness of its thorns. Afterward, that series of dreams (which had lasted many years) stopped completely.

Rather than looking only for causes of my discomfort (abuse history, childhood trauma, oedipal complex, etc.), process work helped me to see that the dreams depicting this discomfort were inviting me to follow them in the direction of my wholeness. The dreams that had terrified me were really trying to show me a bigger picture than I was willing or able to see. Once my attitude changed, the dreams did as well. That which I had considered to be a problem was actually my teacher.

Jung said that we are always dreaming, not just when we sleep. Mindell takes this a step further by seeing body symptoms, relationship difficulties, even world conflicts—really, all of our experiences—as manifestations of a dreaming process that patterns our lives. This dreaming process has something to teach us about our wholeness, bringing to our attention (if we allow it) all that is peripheral, excluded, denied, rejected, or despised. We can choose to become aware of this process and learn from it, or we can ignore or fight against it. In my experience—and in the experience of my friends, colleagues, clients, and students—following the dreaming process makes life richer, fuller, and more meaningful.

Following Experiences to the Mystery

In order to go along with the Tao (or the dreaming process), we have to know the direction of its flow. Lao Tsu helps us understand how to do this.

> *The Tao that can be told*
> *is not the eternal Tao ....*
>
> *The unnamable is eternally real.*
> *Naming is the origin*
> *of all particular things ...*
> *Yet mystery and manifestations*
> *arise from the same source.*

There are two kinds of Tao. One is the Tao that can be told—that which we can name—the 10,000 things. The other is the unnamable, the mystery itself, the origin of Heaven and Earth. Yet both of these, mystery and manifestation, arise from the same source. Lao Tsu goes on to say:

> *In the beginning was the Tao.*
> *All things issue from it;*
> *all things return to it.*
>
> *To find the origin,*
> *trace back the manifestations.*
> *When you recognize the children*
> *and find the mother,*
> *you will be free of sorrow.*

In this fascinating passage, we learn that by tracing back its manifestations, we can find the Tao itself. The ancient Taoists studied Nature empirically (observing the manifestations) in order to discover the Tao, so they could live in harmony with it. It's the same with process work. Everything we experience is a manifestation of the dreaming process. When we follow our experiences and unfold them, then we can trace them back to the process itself. Like the Taoist, the process worker studies phenomena in order to follow Nature. She learns to carefully observe herself and the people with whom she works so she can notice the direction in which the process is naturally flowing and help it to flow there.

Remember Sharon and Tomasz. By noticing and following what was naturally happening when they played, we found the direction that their music was trying to go. We traced the manifestations back to the process itself, to discover what Nature wanted them to play.

What is this Nature? Is it in us? Is it outside of us? Is it in the music itself? I honestly don't know. I do know, though, after witnessing thousands of such experiences, that when people notice and follow what actually happens when they play, they get to something deeper, more real, and more exciting than their normal way of playing. The Taoists tell us to find the Tao, the force from which everything springs, and align ourselves with it. My guess is that by noticing and following what happens when we are creative, we find our way back to the creative source itself. When we step back and let *it* play, we align ourselves with that deeper creativity.

For me, Taoism is an attitude. It is about saying yes to what is, and discovering the amazing things that happen to our music and creativity when we do that. But what does it mean to say yes to what is? There are 10,000 things that occur when someone picks up an instrument, opens her mouth to sing, picks up a paintbrush, puts pen to paper, or does anything creative. In order to decide what part of your music, your art, or yourself to support, it will be useful to have a few more concepts under your belt. Please remember that this is not theory for its own sake. Rather, the ideas I am about to share will help you to follow and unfold the mystery.

Who Am I, Anyway?

Jung taught us that dreams point us toward our wholeness, pull us in directions that we may not otherwise go, and compensate our normal attitudes about ourselves and the world. Since, as he also said, we are always dreaming, it follows that many of our experiences have these same functions. How does this work? A diagram might help to clarify.

See chart 1. This is a picture of me. That box includes my entire identity as a man, singer, process worker, teacher, American, and on and on. Everything that I think of as me is inside that box. The x's around the box are things that I consider to be "not-me." For instance, those x's might represent a dream that scared me, a body symptom I would rather get rid of, the elderly woman next door who screams at spirits in her apartment in the middle of the night, and the terrible things I read in the newspaper.

31

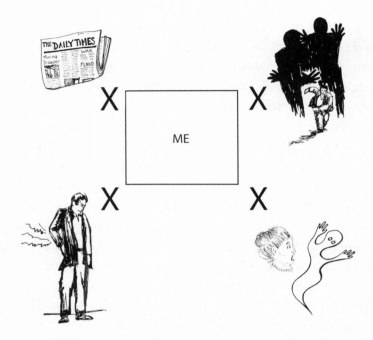

Chart 1. This chart is a picture of me. Everything I think of as "me" is inside the box. The x's represent things I consider to be "not me."

Now let's say that I take a different perspective and realize that the dream, like my dream of the menacing men, is actually an expression of a part of me that I was not aware of. Instead of being scared of it, instead of thinking that those huge men are *not* me, I expand my identity and embrace the dream and what it represents. Suddenly the picture changes.

See chart 2. The box around my identity has grown. I have taken a step in the direction of my wholeness. You can see that there is still a box around me. I still experience that symptom and my neighbor as not me.

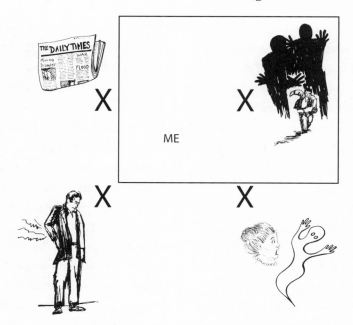

ME

Chart 2. This chart shows how we develop toward whole-ness when we embrace the things we normally think of as "not me." The box around my identity has grown to include the huge men in my scary dream. I now realize that they, and what they represent, are also part of me.

But wait. As I write here alone in my apartment, day after day and night after night, I catch myself laughing aloud, squealing with delight, or shouting questions to no one in particular. Perhaps I am not so different from my neighbor, after all. Whoops! That box just got bigger again.

Primary and Secondary Processes

In process work, my sense of "me" is called the primary process and all the things that I consider to be "not-me" are called secondary processes. The primary process is defined not only by my identity but also by my awareness, by the things I do, and by my intention. That means that the things I experience as not-me are secondary, as are things that I have less awareness of, things that happen to me, and those that happen unintentionally.

Why do we need to differentiate between primary and secondary experiences? Because we are trying to get in touch with the dreaming process, which is continually pulling us towards change and development. If we want to know the direction it is moving, we first have to know where we are. Then we can notice which experiences challenge our identity and intentions, and we can learn from those experiences and align ourselves with the flow of process. Let's see what this has to do with music.

A huge banging from a construction site outside the window disturbed my work with a classical pianist. He wanted help with his interpretation of a piece, but it was nearly impossible to hear what he was playing. We were both exasperated. Then I remembered that the not-me is an indication of a secondary process. The sledge-hammers were as far from the pianist's identity as could be. So he was shy when I suggested that he incorporate the quality of that crashing in his music. He was used to playing smoothly, at an even volume. But as he banged on the keys in time with the workers outside, the piece became not only louder, but more dynamic, rhythmic, energetic, powerful. He started to enjoy this way of playing, and eventually got swept up in the tidal wave of music that rushed through him. He had found his interpretation, and was no longer in the least bit distracted by the continued banging outside.

A guitar player sat with me in the middle of the circle during a seminar. As we waited for the other participants to settle down so that we could begin, I noticed him gently pressing and releasing the strings of his guitar with the fingers of his left hand, producing an almost inaudible chord. When we officially started working, he played quite loudly, strumming vigorously with his right hand. I called his attention to what had happened before he played. He had not been aware of doing that (which indicated that it was secondary).

I asked him to play the same song without using his right hand at all, just by pressing the chords on the strings with his left hand. Where there had been a room full of continuous, loud sound, there were now soft chords with pauses between them. He said that he could feel the music in his belly, which stirred up many emotions. This quiet feeling state was a new experience for him. When he played again, this time using both hands, he was touched by the music's sensitivity.

A singer could not reach the high note of an aria. As the melody rose, she felt a pressure in her chest, constricting her and cutting off the sound. (She was not creating the pressure on purpose. Rather, she was the "victim" of it, meaning that it was secondary.) I asked her to make that same pressure on my chest. She pushed me hard with her hands, digging her feet into the ground and using all of her strength. I had to really struggle to hold my ground. I suggested that she sing the difficult passage while pushing me in this way. For some reason, she was able to hit the high note without a problem. Then she pushed against the wall and sang, also successfully.

Soon it was possible for her to feel that same power, and reach the same note, simply standing still and feeling her feet pressing into the ground. Finally, she was able to sing the whole aria without tension or undue strain, just by remembering and trusting the power inside herself. After the session, she told me that she also needed to use that inner strength when her boyfriend acted domineering, rather than letting herself be pushed around.

Another pianist had a problem with a complicated, very fast passage in a piece by Chopin. He said that his playing sounded unclear and messy. (This messiness happened against his wishes, and so was a secondary process.) I recommended that he play it even less clearly. When he did, he realized that his whole arm was shaking. When he then shook his arm intentionally, he found that it was easier to play the passage. He had been trying to play with his fingers, but could not move them so quickly. When he shook his entire arm, he could play the rhythm without difficulty, and it freed his fingers to merely be in position for the correct notes. They did not have to raise and lower themselves, since this was accomplished by his arm. Paradoxically, the pianist had to let himself be *messy* in order to learn to play *clearly*. Like Lao Tsu would say

> *If you want to become straight,*
> *Let yourself be crooked ...*
> *If you want to get rid of something,*
> *you must first allow it to flourish.*

A Fluid Identity

So, you might ask, once I notice the secondary process, realize it is also me, and start to live my life—or play music—in a way that embraces this new way of being, I'm done, right? No, because the process is always changing. The moment I embrace the secondary process, I have created a new identity. Other experiences arise that are not a part of that new identity, experiences of which I am not yet fully aware, or that disturb me or go against my intentions. The picture really looks something like this (see chart 3).

Of course, none of these drawings is really accurate. To paraphrase Lao Tsu, the process that can be drawn is not the true process. There are infinite ways in which processes can flow and change. But this is supposed to be a picture of a dynamically changing identity, constantly in flux between primary and secondary, continually growing and transforming and discovering new parts of itself. This is the Taoist who follows Nature wherever it leads her. She is a leaf blown by the wind. Then she becomes the wind itself and blows to her heart's content, until she comes to a wall that

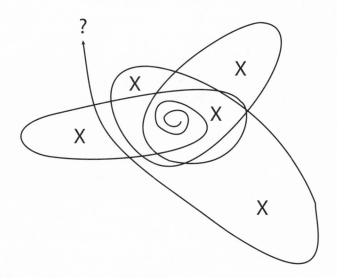

Chart 3. This chart represents a fluid identity. The "me" has embraced various qualities and aspects that were previously considered to be "not me." In this way, the identity dynamically grows and transforms. As the next secondary process arises, it is, in turn, included in this constantly changing sense of "who I am in this moment." The question mark shows that it is impossible to know what new secondary process will arise, or how my identity will grow in the future.

stops her. So she becomes the wall and enjoys its stability for a while. She is not disturbed by anything for long, because everything that disturbs her becomes her teacher. She is fluid between her different parts, open to discovering new vistas or revisiting places she had once called home but are now foreign to her. She has discarded the boat and become the river.

Channels

The dreaming process expresses itself in many different ways. Movement was an important part of the messy pianist's process. If we had worked just with the sound of his music, we would have missed his shaking arms. The feelings in the guitarist's belly were key to his process. The singer's process started with the feeling of pressure and shifted to movement as she pushed against me. By helping us be aware of how we perceive, the idea of *channels* helps us to notice where the dreaming process is expressing itself in each moment.

As I look at the screen of my computer, I am using the visual channel. My fingers move (movement channel) across the keys. The tips of my fingers feel (body-feeling channel) the hardness of the keys while my stomach feels (also body-feeling channel) full from the meal I have just eaten. I hear (auditory channel) the clicks of the keys. Words and sentences (verbal channel) form in my mind and on the screen. I am writing to you, dear reader (relationship channel), and hoping that this book makes an impact on the world (world channel).

Like our experiences, the ways in which we perceive are also structured by our identity and intentions. An example: I see a tree outside my window. I hear the rustle of its leaves and I see its branches swaying in the wind. Aha! I am seeing and hearing, but the tree is moving. I don't want to move now. I want to write this chapter. I am identified with the visual, auditory, and verbal channels. I am not identified with the movement channel. Another way of saying this is that my visual, auditory, and verbal channels are momentarily occupied, while my movement channel is now unoccupied.

What does it really mean if a channel is occupied or not? For instance, I am sitting in a chair. That means my chair is now occupied. When I stand up, the chair is unoccupied, right? Well, if you were here, you would see that my chair is still occupied—by a cushion. It is the same with channel occupation. When "I" am not occupying a channel, that channel is not necessarily empty. It is occupied by something that is not-me.

For instance, my movement channel is unoccupied in the moment, but that does not mean it is empty. The tree is there, in the movement channel, swaying in the wind. The fact that a channel is unoccupied often means that something interesting and unknown is happening there. *The juicy stuff almost always happens in unoccupied channels.* That is where our secondary processes hang out. As a result, entering the unoccupied channel and allowing it to express itself is usually a sure-fire way to follow the dreaming process.

Now I am standing. My body starts to move with the tree, gently rocking, straightening, and yet again swaying. I love the combination of stillness in movement. The tree—or is it me?—is rooted in the earth yet always dancing.

Try This:

1. How would you describe yourself? Focus on your qualities, not the things you do. What are you like? Write down some key words that you can readily identify with.

2. What or who disturbs you? You might want to think about people you know, or something you dreamed, or a body problem that you would like to get rid of. Write them down.

3. Choose one of the things you wrote in #2. Write down some key words that describe that person or thing. Try to notice the qualities of that person or thing, rather than your personal feelings and reactions. (For instance, instead of writing that my neighbor is crazy and always wakes me up in the middle of the night with her screams, I would write that she is loud, sudden, seemingly irrational, and does not conform to societal rules.) Try to be as specific as possible with your description.

4. Just for a moment, try to identify with the qualities in #3. This does not mean that you have to become exactly like the person or thing that disturbs you. Rather, take on and identify with those qualities.

5. Experiment with making music or doing something creative with those qualities. Let them play or create. Keep doing it until you find something you like about that music or art.

Chapter 3

"It's All Right!"
Metaskills

When you walk down the street, do you hear cars and buses? Horns and screeching tires? Birds and people? Or do you hear a symphony? Bend your ear right now. Listen to the sounds around you. There must be sounds, even if you are in a quiet room.

Try to imagine that you are a baby who doesn't know where those sounds come from. You don't know that the dog is breathing. You just hear a sound. You don't know that your neighbor is taking a shower. You just hear a sound. Now bend your ear again. Imagine that your room is a concert hall. And all those sounds around you are notes and rhythms of a new kind of music. Don't listen to the refrigerator. Listen to the low hum coming from that large metal instrument in your kitchen. That is music. Hear the rustle of paper as you turn the page. What a beautiful sound. Now read this sentence out loud. Don't pay attention to the words but instead listen to the quality of your voice. Is it quiet or loud? Is it melodic, or do all the words have the same pitch? Read this sentence out loud and listen again.

This is music. You are not reading but singing. Every time you open your mouth you are singing; you just don't know it. Every time you walk across the room, you play a rhythm on the drum that is your floor. Can you hear it? Listen again to the sounds out-side. There *is* a symphony out there.

Basho, the wandering 17th-century Japanese Zen monk and haiku master, heard in such a way.

> *Sparrows in the eaves,*
> *mice in the ceiling—*
> *celestial music.*

Now try listening with the same open ears to the music that you and other people play. Stop hearing what you expect to be there, and instead enjoy what *is*. Open not just your ears but your heart and your mind to it. Let your whole being breathe it in like the fresh scent of a mountain breeze. While you're at it, why not have the same attitude toward yourself? Just for a moment, try being open to who you are, rather than who you expect yourself to be. Enjoy your-self. Even those things you normally hate. What a relief.

What Tomasz remembered (in chapter 1) as being helpful in our work was a look in my eye, an unspoken message of accept-ance—not anything I did. Your attitudes toward yourself, people, and music are as important as—if not more important than—the methods you use to work with unintentional music. Amy Mindell tried to find out why certain therapists are more effective than oth-ers. She noticed that their feeling attitudes, not just their skills, made them more helpful to their clients. She called these feeling attitudes metaskills. Whether you plan to explore your own unin-tentional music and creativity, or to help other people discover theirs, your metaskills will be essential.

A Loving Attitude Conquers Criticism

Rainer Maria Rilke, the great poet of the 19th and early 20th centuries, was a wellspring of metaskills. In his *Letters to a Young*

Poet, he models an inspiring attitude about art, artists, and the creative process. Rilke refuses to critique the poems of his young correspondent, saying that "nothing touches a work of art so little as words of criticism." He goes on to say that "only love can touch and hold [works of art] and be fair to them." These are welcome words for anyone who has put herself on the line and played music in front of another person. The specter of criticism can make playing in a concert, or even at a gathering of friends, a daunting experience. There were times my own inner critic stopped me from singing even when alone. Some music teachers unwittingly contribute to this pain. With the best intentions, they teach us the "correct" way to play rather than help us to find our own individual access to music. Rather than love, they offer criticism to guide us down the path they have already followed.

Undoubtedly, this can be helpful for many. Some people thrive when given straight feedback. But criticism can also be painful, regardless of your level of musical achievement. And it is most acutely felt by children. I have heard countless horror stories from people who never sing or play because some family member or teacher criticized their first attempts.

I remember working with one such woman in a seminar. Cecile had grown up in a family of singers and was made to sing in her mother's choir at a young age. But she was soon thrown out because she sang off pitch. After that, her mother often scolded her for this "defect" and said to others that she could not imagine how any daughter of hers could sing so poorly. Cecile was traumatized by the public humiliation and never sang again.

Cecile looked terrified when she stepped into the center of the circle. She spoke very quietly, nervously glancing at the other participants. Although she was angry with her mother, it was clear that she inwardly agreed that singing out of tune was unacceptable. As we brainstormed about how to work with this problem, Cecile hit on the idea that she could sing a song with the whole group. (That was, in and of itself, an enormous step for her.) Singing all together had two advantages. She would not have to sing alone in front of all those people; and it would be a kind of reenactment of her painful choir experience. A reenactment with a twist.

We agreed on a children's song that everyone knew. As expected, Cecile drifted from the notes the rest of the group was singing. Gently encouraging this drifting, I asked her to sing whatever melody she felt was correct. I sang with her, accenting the "wrong" notes. When she sang too high, I sang even higher. This helped her to stray further from the melody of the song. At one point she held a note too long, and another not long enough. At each "mistake," I made my notes even longer or shorter than hers. Soon the group had stopped singing and the two of us were doing a strange, almost atonal improvisation that was fun and dynamic. Our song ranged from high squeaks to low roars, from long tones to bursts of staccato rhythm. When she started to move and make faces, our music became a dance and a performance as well.

Afterwards Cecile was jubilant. She said she had never in her life enjoyed singing until that moment. The work did not help her to sing on pitch. But it did unlock a playful, joyous, and creative musical spirit. Criticism had frozen her at an early age. As Rilke would say, only love—or a loving attitude toward what she described as her inability to sing on pitch—could touch and hold and be fair to the fledgling singer inside of her.

Curiosity And Awe

When I hear some otherwise unwanted or unloved aspect of someone's music—like Cecile's wandering pitch—a strange thing happens inside of me. I get insanely curious. Her mother hated it. She hates it. Everyone wants to get rid of it. How fascinating. What process, what potential music, could possibly be behind that disturbing and irrational sound? I can hardly wait to witness the metamorphosis into . . . who knows what? It's impossible to predict. Who could have imagined that Cecile's "defect" would evolve into an avant-garde improvisation?

Every sound, every piece of music, every stroke of color, every word on a page, every step across a stage, every person in every moment leads us in unexpected directions and into unknown territory. I'm filled with awe when faced with that mystery. My whole being feels like the wide eyes of a child seeing the ocean for the first time. Every day. And that sense of wonder seems to give people permission to be themselves.

Courage and Trust

Encouraging disturbing or irrational phenomena is a radical act. It takes a warrior's courage. Rilke reassures us here. "This is in the end the only kind of courage that is required of us: the courage to face the strangest, most unusual, most inexplicable experiences that can meet us." Where do we find such courage? Most of us live comfortably in our normal world and are terrified of the strange, the inexplicable. How can we meet it, face it, welcome it, even encourage it? Rilke helps us once again. "You must realize that something is happening to you, that life has not forgotten you, that it holds you in its hand and will not let you fall." We could call this having faith in the wisdom of the process. Rilke says it so beautifully. Life holds you in its hand and will not let you fall.

Remember back to Sharon who, after a few minutes of following her unintentional music, could no longer make a sound with her flute. In that moment of doubt, I remembered Rilke's words and waited calmly for whatever would happen next. As he says, we should stand "confidently in the storms of spring, not afraid that afterward summer may not come. It does come." Such strange experiences change into beautiful (or, at the very least, meaningful) experiences when given the right kind of attention. "What now appears to us as the most alien will become our most intimate and trusted experience ... Perhaps everything that frightens us is, in its deepest essence, something helpless that wants our love."

We have come full circle. In order to transform alien and disturbing experiences into intimate and trusted ones, we must give them love. To do that, we must have the courage to meet these experiences. This courage comes from knowing that they will change, that spring storms will turn to summer warmth, that life has not forgotten us and will not let us fall. Courage, trust, and love. These are metaskills that can help us with our music and creativity, as well as help us when working with others as they make music or art. And a good dollop of curiosity keeps the skin tingling.

A Loving, Deep Democracy

The point is not to embrace unintentional music and abandon your original way of playing. That would be like a revolution where the old order is forced out and replaced by the new. With our music, as in the world, we need a way to facilitate change that does not perpetuate that painful cycle. Mindell coined the phrase "deep democracy" to describe an attitude about the world: that all people and opinions should be represented, allowed to speak and be involved in making decisions that affect our lives. Deep democracy with music would mean valuing everything we play, whether intended or not. It would mean letting all the different parts of us express themselves and influence our musical decisions.

Instead of one dominating or replacing the other, intentional and unintentional can entwine as lovers. Rilke says that the creative act "is essentially *one*, whether it is manifested as mental or physical; for mental creation too arises from the physical, is of one nature with it and only like a softer, more enraptured and more eternal repetition of bodily delight . . . In one creative thought a thousand forgotten nights of love come to life again and fill it with majesty and exaltation." So, too, with the creative interplay between primary and secondary music. This dance of tenderness, of passion, of sweetness, of depth, can be an echo, an inner repetition of the eternal dance of love and birth. It can lead to a new way of making music that can be recognized as the child of both parents, but which is individual and unique. Our newfound style need not replace our old one. But, if they interact as lovers do, giving to each other as well as taking, the result could be a blessing, a newness, an unexpected guest bearing gifts.

I was practicing a ballad alone at home. I'd always heard it sung or played softly, and had always sung it that way myself; so I tried yet again to keep the volume low even when the melody went high. But no matter how much I tried, my voice got louder as the pitch rose. All of those years of voice lessons for nothing, I thought. Then my curiosity started to kick in. Putting aside self-criticism, I trusted the disturbance and let my voice sing the way it wanted to. The song transformed from a sad ballad into a bluesy, heartfelt cry of anguish and longing. It was so different from any interpretation I had heard before, that I couldn't imagine singing it that way in front of people. The quiet melody was so beautiful, so integral to the song's message. I just could not give it up altogether.

Soon after, I sang that song in concert, giving expression to both styles, letting them dance together. Starting out in low tones, I sang the melody simply and tenderly until the music itself started to carry me. Then feelings rose within me, and with them my voice started building to a climax. I was practically wailing, singing higher than my normal range, letting the melody recreate itself. Then, as if cued by some invisible conductor, my voice dropped to a whisper. The band members, who had followed my ecstatic rise with a double-time beat, suddenly fell quiet. Bass and brushes on the snare drum accompanied my final, imploring phrase. I really felt the pain expressed in those words. Embarrassed by my nakedness, I left the stage immediately. A man from the audience thanked me afterwards, saying it had helped him get in touch with his sadness after breaking up with his girlfriend. No one had ever thanked me in the past when I was struggling to sing the song correctly.

Being with What Is

Having learned from the poet Rainer Maria Rilke, let us return to the *Tao Te Ching* in order to discover more metaskills. Lao Tsu writes:

> *When people see some things as beautiful,*
> *other things become ugly.*
> *When people see some things as good,*
> *other things become bad.*

We all have our preferences. But according to Lao Tsu, the very act of seeing something as beautiful makes something else ugly. When working with or playing music, if we prefer one sound over another, hear one as good and another as bad, we limit our ability to support what is happening. What else can we do? Lao Tsu tells us what the sage does:

> *Things arise and she lets them come;*
> *things disappear and she lets them go.*

Rather than judging experiences, just be with what is. That advice was helpful when I worked with Mark, a tenor saxophone player. He was a friend of the woman who had organized a seminar I led in a European city. He didn't come to the seminar but scheduled a session before I left town. A jazz musician in his twenties, Mark seemed curious but skeptical. He didn't have any specific problems he wanted help with. I had the feeling he was there to humor his friend.

When Mark started to play, before any sound came out of his sax, some breath leaked out from around the mouthpiece. Doing this again with more awareness, Mark blew for a couple of seconds and then a tone came. As he tried it even more, there was nothing audible at first and then a very loud and sudden sound. He experienced this first as waiting and then as an explosion. It was an intense experience for him. He said it was not just an explosion of sound, but also an explosion of emotions coming up from inside of him. But at the same time, he had a feeling in his throat of being cut off. He demonstrated this by making a sudden movement with his hand as if he were chopping his throat, and letting out a quick, "Zack!" It seemed he had gotten to an edge. Something was stopping him from exploding.

I encouraged him to go back to that intense moment, but he said that the explosion was not music, that he could not impose all those feelings on others. I tried again to convince him, but he wanted to focus on the feeling in his throat, since he had often experienced that as a disturbing symptom when he played.

Mark felt that some things are music, and some things are not. Like the people described by Lao Tsu, he was attached to certain sounds and judged others to be ugly. I thought the explosion was new, exciting, and could potentially transform his music. But Mark himself was not interested in it. In any case, he could not explode because something was cutting off his throat. Lao Tsu says, when something arises, let it come; when it disappears, let it go. So I let go of my attachment to the explosion and followed the next thing that had arisen, namely the feeling in his throat.

Mark said that when this feeling comes as he plays, he usually just pushes through it. I encouraged him to feel it more. He did, and repeated the motion of chopping. We set up a role-play in which he became "the chopper" and I took the role of "Mark." As his hand hit the pillow near my throat, he said, "Stop playing!" I said, "No, I want to play! I like to play!" He just hit it again and repeated, "Stop!" (This surprised me. I had guessed that the "Zack!" would turn into a loud sound, that the hit would get bigger and bigger and we would be back to the explosion. Once again, I had to let go of my expectation.)

He had no associations to this stopper. It did not remind him of anyone from his life. He said it just wanted him to stop playing for a moment. I suggested that he simply stop playing sometimes. He looked at me like I was crazy and said that would be impossible. People come to hear him play concerts of free jazz, and he feels that he has to play all the time during his concerts. That is a part of his style; it is expected of him. I laughed and said that he plays free jazz but he feels totally unfree. I said that people come to a free jazz concert in part so they can learn to be free, and that he could model that by being free enough to sometimes not play. That intrigued him. Picking up his sax, Mark started to experiment with playing and stopping. He built his improvisation around complex modal lines, unexpected pauses, and long silences. The holes in the sound created an almost architectural feeling of space, framing his musical ideas, contributing to them.

When he finished, Mark told me that he had not experienced that feeling in his throat. Since he kept stopping, the muscles were not tense or overtaxed. The pauses also gave him a chance to think about what he would say next. Usually, he said, it all goes by too quickly for him to think. And, he added almost reluctantly, the music was kind of cool.

There is an interesting contrast between what happened here and the outcome of Tomasz's process. Tomasz learned not to *think* about what he would play before he played it, while Mark was happy to finally have a *moment to reflect on* his next phrase. Like a dream that compensates a one-sided attitude about life, unintentional music balances a one-sided musical attitude. Tomasz was too concerned with building a structure; Mark was identified with being free, unstructured, and producing nonstop music. It is not surprising that their unintentional music led them in opposite directions.

Mark may eventually find out about explosions and all those feelings that he said he cannot impose on the audience. Or maybe he won't. In any case, that afternoon was definitely not the time for it. If I had continued in that direction, Mark would have been justifiably upset with me for trying to push him into big sounds and big emotions. Our work would have stalled and nothing would have come out of it except bad feelings on both sides. So I dropped my preference and simply followed what was present. Once again, we see the wisdom of Lao Tsu:

> *A good traveler has no fixed plans*
> *and is not intent upon arriving ...*
> *A good scientist has freed himself of concepts*
> *and keeps his mind open to what is.*

It is not always easy to live these metaskills. At a certain point in the work, I thought Mark had a problem. In my opinion, he was judging the explosion and attached to the stopper. But really I was the same as Mark. I was, just as much as he, judging one side of the dynamic and attached to the other. Luckily, the process itself teaches you what to do. You have an idea, but the stupid musician won't follow you. Then you realize that the musician's process is wise and you have to let go of your concept and open up to what is.

A Jazz Sage

I saw an interview once with a piano player who used to play with Miles Davis, the late, great jazz trumpet player. He told of a certain concert in which he made a mistake and played the wrong chord on the piano. Miles played notes that made the chord sound right. When the pianist heard that, he could not play any more. He just sat there with his mouth hanging open, amazed at what this genius had done. He explained to the interviewer that, for Miles, whatever was played was reality. You have to deal with that. You cannot play along with what should be played. You have to play with what is played.

This not only demonstrates an awesome musical ability, but it is also a spiritual teaching for all of life. Many of us are concerned with what should happen, and if what we expect and want does not occur, we are lost, afraid, or angry. Miles would just say, that is the reality. Deal with it. Play with it.

Try This:

1. Close your eyes and listen to the sounds inside you and all around you. Listen like a baby, or like a visitor to this planet who has never heard those sounds before. If you hear your-self thinking, don't listen to the words themselves, but instead listen to the voice that is talking in your head. Is the voice high or low? Is it loud or soft? Do the words come quickly or slowly? If you hear a melody, listen to its essential quality as if you have never heard it before. If you hear a car, a dripping tap, your neighbors fighting, or a ringing in your ears, just listen to the sounds themselves, as if they were music.

2. When you are ready, pick one of those sounds and sing it to yourself or reproduce it somehow. You can do it loudly or so quietly that no one else would be able to hear you. But make sure you can hear yourself.

3. Now listen to the sound you are making. Try to be open to it. Love it. Caress each sound with a tender embrace. Sing it again and again. That is music.

4. If you want, feel free to add to the rhythm or add another note in the same style. But don't go away from the basic quality of your original sound.

5. Enjoy your new song.

6. You can try this same experiment with friends. Take five minutes to listen before each of you starts to sing your own music. Notice how different each person's song is, or how

similar. Try holding on to your own music in spite of every-thing else you hear. Then try blending your song with theirs. If someone else's music attracts you, sing it for a while. If someone's music repels you, try singing that, too. Maybe you'll find that you like it. Remember that all this music was already there, inside and outside of you.

Part II

Counterpoint

*"When Allen Ginsberg was asked, 'Were the Beats first
and foremost artists or first and foremost spiritual
seekers?' he saw the trap and refused to enter. The two,
he answered, are inseparable, and he cited the example
of the Milarepa school of Tibetan Buddhism, where in
order to become a lama one must reportedly also be an
archer, a calligrapher, or a poet."*

–Stephen Prothero

Chapter 4

Is This Self-Discovery?

I don't like the word *psychology*. It summons up images of people in white coats watching rats run through mazes. Of silent men with white beards listening to patients who lie on couches. Of diagnoses and getting rid of problems. When I tell people at parties that I'm a therapist, they usually take a step back. They are afraid I will analyze them or that I can discover their secrets just by watching them.

Many musicians, like others in the creative arts, don't want to have anything to do with therapy. They are afraid that looking too deeply at what is inside will take away their creative impulses. For many artists, creating is like a madness. If therapy makes them normal, then their art might suffer. Some feel they are "taken over" by someone or something that creates. It is not they who work; this other thing does. They fear that therapy could take that away. Musicians and other artists want their daemons and demons in pure, unadulterated form.

This aversion to therapy may be, in part, a reaction to early and influential psychological theories about art. Freud thought of creativity as one manifestation of a defense mechanism he called sublimation. He believed that we channel our unconscious sexual or aggressive energies into culturally approved behaviors, like art or music. This perspective seems to suggest that if you analyze and work through your sexual and aggressive energies to the extent that you no longer need to defend against them, then the sublimation—and, therefore, the creativity—would stop.

Such a viewpoint also harbors a subtle judgment that creativity is not something valuable in its own right but, rather, a byproduct of some other psychological process that keeps us from unleashing our unconsciousness into the world. This hint of judgment continues in Freud's understanding of creativity as, in part, "an undue perpetuation of childhood play." Does this mean that if we were truly adult, then we would have no need for such childishness? If this were the case, then I would not want to delve too deeply into my psyche for fear that either my creative impulses would abandon me or that I, seeing their true nature, would drop them as I did my other childhood toys. I, for one, would rather play music than have this type of insight.

Jung, on the other hand, saw creativity as flowing directly from the "living fountain of instinct," and said the unconscious "is the very source of the creative impulse." This vastly different attitude has equally different ramifications. In Jung's view, if we contact our deepest selves then we find the spring from which our creativity issues. This brings to mind "Kubla Khan," that wonderful poem by Samuel Taylor Coleridge, which many have understood to be a vision of the creative process.

> *And from this chasm, with ceaseless turmoil seething,*
> *As if this earth in fast thick pants were breathing,*
> *A mighty fountain momently was forced:*
> *Amid whose swift half-intermitted burst*
> *Huge fragments vaulted like rebounding hail,*
> *Or chaffy grain beneath the thresher's flail:*
> *And mid these dancing rocks at once and ever*
> *It flung up momently the sacred river.*

For Coleridge, as for Jung, the river from which our creativity emerges is a sacred one, itself a living and breathing entity. Its ceaseless turmoil brings to the surface, from deep hidden recesses, huge fragments that, like grain beneath a thresher's flail, are potentially nourishing to our souls. We could say that the river is process itself, the eternal mystery that flows in and around all of us.

We need not fear analyzing away our creativity. The river of process is the very source of that creativity. We need not fear becoming too normal. We might, in fact, get stranger than we were before, like the ecstatic poet in "Kubla Khan." ("His flashing eyes/his floating hair!") We need not fear that we will no longer be "taken over" by our daemons. Process work invites our daemons, helps us to step aside as they do their magic, teaches us to find them when they are hiding rather than wait patiently for inspiration. Delving inside and contacting the sacred river only enhances our creativity. Creating, in turn, becomes an important part of the sacred work of self-discovery.

I do not use the word *sacred* lightly. For me personally, process work is a spiritual practice. It helps me to get in touch with the deepest part of myself and to recognize it in others. It helps me to wake up to who I am and to be open to who I am becoming. Process work helps me to go beyond what is known, allowing me to dance with that undiscovered essence that lives and breathes just over that line. It puts me in touch with something larger than myself—something that shapes me and moves me and gives my life meaning.

Music is an inextricable part of my own growth and change and, by extension, of the process work I do with others. I am unabashedly devoted to those unintentional sounds that shatter the shells of our current identities and pull us in new and exciting directions, coaxing us in the direction of our wholeness.

Slouching Toward Stillness

James, a teenage guitar student of mine, showed up for one of my seminars wearing a leather jacket and ripped jeans. He wanted to know what "weird stuff" I was doing with musicians, but I could tell he was wondering whether he should have bothered. He sat slouched against the wall, looking out suspiciously from under his unwashed hair at the strange "therapy-type" people all around him. Finally, it was his turn to work.

Playing a Jimi Hendrix song I had taught him, he lingered too long on a certain chord. I told him that he had made a mistake and asked him to start over. To my surprise, he made the same mistake again and could not correct it even after I reminded him a third time of the "right" rhythm. Finally waking up from my "guitar teacher" role and remembering why we were there, I encouraged James to hold the chord for as long as he wished. He played the chord for a very long time, strumming again and again, softly and slowly. When his eyelids started lowering, I suggested he close them altogether. His breathing slowed and deepened. I placed my hands on his back around his ribs and pressed gently, to help him be aware of the expansion and contraction of his lungs.

When he finally opened his eyes, he told me that he had gone deep inside in a kind of meditation, something he had never done before. I could tell by his half-lowered lids, quiet voice, and calm demeanor that something in him had shifted. The rhythmic "mistake" was the beginning of an inner journey of self-discovery that continues to this day. (He is also now the rhythm guitarist in a speed-metal band.)

Schubert and the Cosmic Joke

When you play music, who is really playing? Is it only you? Or is someone else in there, peeking through, squeaking out, shouting in the background, getting caught in your throat and putting her own twist on the music that you think is yours? Perhaps your dreams are leaking into that song. Why not? Your dreams are in your body, in your relationships. They are everywhere you look and especially in those places you don't look. So when you unfold unintentional music, chances are you'll end up right in the middle of your dreaming process.

I had never met Elaine before she asked me for a session. She was in Portland, Oregon, for a few weeks in order to take part in some classes. Since I had no piano, and hers was in another city, Elaine found and rented a practice room at a local university. A warm, powerfully built woman with grown children, she struck me as someone who knows exactly what she wants and then makes sure she gets it.

Elaine sat down at the piano and played a piece by Schubert. Certain notes (the first and third beat of each measure) were a little louder and faster than the rest. When she exaggerated this at my suggestion, she really enjoyed it, saying that it freed her up and allowed her to "get into" the piano more. Getting into the piano even more, she played a wrong note. She played the mistake again and smiled slightly. She said that playing in that way had made her laugh inside, that it was like a joke. I encouraged her to play the entire piece as if it were a joke.

She did this by making very subtle mistakes—a wrong note here, but not wrong enough to really notice, a strange harmony there, but not that strange. She told me that this was meant to make me uncomfortable and uncertain. I was not supposed to know which notes and chords were right and which were wrong. She said that uncertainty, the grain of doubt, was the source of humor.

I told her I did not find the original piece at all funny. She agreed, saying it was rigid and regimented. I observed that two distinct personalities or two outlooks on life seemed to be emerging—one that was strict and regimented, the other full of uncertainty and humor. At this, her jaw dropped. This conflict dominated her entire life, she said.

We had been working together for about fifteen minutes and already we had hit upon Elaine's core issue.

She said that she tried to be certain about every aspect of life, and that unexpected events made her—and everyone else—very uncomfortable. Her father had taught her to obey the law and to value order. I thought to myself that since Elaine wanted to be certain, this was closer to her identity and intentions. Her father's values, which had influenced her at an early age, were by now a part of her own belief system. By embracing law and order, she made sure that everything stayed predictable. This kept her from crossing her edge into uncertainty.

I asked Elaine what she thought about jokes. She said that jokes were fine, but that one could not joke about things that hurt people. But then she was not sure about that, saying that sometimes jokes are about hurting people. She said that one should not joke about certain topics, and then took that back as well. I pointed out that she was trying to make a rigid system about joking, but that things were not so certain. She laughed, realizing that she was setting up laws even about humor.

She spent her life trying to make sure everything was in place, she said, but there was always something uncertain, and the greatest uncertainty was death. She compared this dilemma to Buster Keaton trying to get all the ducks in line, but one duck always walked away. She said that this was the cosmic joke. I suggested that if Elaine took part in the joke, by noticing what was out of line and pushing it ever so slightly further from the line, then she would no longer be the butt of the joke but the joker. This is what she had done when she made me uncertain with her music. Smiling broadly, she said this made her feel like a trickster, and that her favorite myths were about Hermes and other tricksters.

It seemed we had tapped into Elaine's life myth. To check whether this was true, I asked whether she remembered a childhood dream. She told me that the following dream had repeatedly come to her when she was a child: She was in her bed in her parent's house, and there were four figures running up and down the hall outside her room. They were all wrapped in gauze like mummies and they ran back and forth through the hall. They ran into the closet and fell all over each other and then got up and ran back and forth again, and then back to the closet where they fell over each other again. She was terrified in the dream because she thought they were coming to get her.

Childhood dreams point to life myths, long-term mythical patterns that structure who we are. They are the rough sketches of the stories we are in the middle of acting out. Throughout her life, Elaine wanted everything to be certain, and she set up rules to leave no doubts. Yet she dreamed of bungling figures who ran to and fro. They fell in an unruly heap in the closet of her parent's house (not conforming to the rigid compartments in which her father, and later Elaine herself, tried to contain and order the world). Wrapped up like mummies, they hinted at death, the greatest uncertainty. To us they seem comical, but they petrified her, for they threatened her long-term primary process.

The part of a childhood dream that we fear often represents the aspect of our myth that is most difficult for us to integrate. It is that part of ourselves that we take our whole lives to become. We could call it the ally, an awesome spirit or energy that plagues us and terrifies us but can potentially help us and guide us through life. As we talked about the dream, Elaine realized for the first time that those slapstick mummies could be her friends and teachers. She grinned mischievously as she talked about how much freer she would feel—and how much more fun life could be—if she loosened the strict limits she had imposed on herself, instead of always defending against the whims of chance and change. She said it was as if her old friend Hermes, the trickster who leads souls to and from the Underworld, was letting her in on the cosmic joke.

All of this was present in her music. Elaine chose a rigid and structured piece—or we could say that her primary identity chose the piece. Her unintentional music made a joke of this serious-ness, just as the mummies made a joke of the seriousness of death. Elaine was pulled to be the slyly smiling creator of uncertainty. She became the one who throws the dice, keeping me in an uncom-fortable suspense about how they would land. For that moment, Elaine had become her own hilarious and unpredictable ally.

Ode to Hermes

O Muses, let us sing now of Hermes, son of Maia and Zeus, messenger of the gods: how he, when not yet a day old, created the lyre; how he stole the cattle of Apollo who shoots from afar, and then charmed the furious god with sweet song; how he created, too, the pipes of Pan from plucked up reeds; how he leads souls down to Hades with as much grace as he flies to Olympus to con-sort with his kin; how he traverses all borders like the thief that he is; how he can teach us about music and life and laughter with his tricky ways.

Elaine's story gives me an excuse to rhapsodize about my favorite mythological figure. The spirit of Hermes guides and inspires this book. A few words about his deeds and their signifi-cance will take us on a short detour that will lead us straight back to our main theme.

On the day he was born, the infant Hermes climbed out of his cradle and happened upon an unfortunate tortoise, which he hol-lowed out and made into the first lyre. The next day, when caught red-handed with Apollo's cattle, Hermes' music turned the heart of the murderous sun god, who delightedly gave him the sacred cows that had been the cause of their dispute. Hermes, in return, gave the lyre to Apollo, who was thereafter known as the god of music.

The god Thoth, who is considered to be the Egyptian parallel to Hermes, was also said to have created the lyre out of the shell of a tortoise. Is this just a coincidence? In ancient China, the oracles obtained from the *I Ching* were recorded on tortoise shells. Another age-old method of divination in China was to heat tortoise shells until they cracked, and to make predictions depending on the patterns formed by the cracks. Could Hermes' instrument somehow be connected with divination?

In the *Homeric Hymn to Hermes,* the tricky god himself speaks of the lyre as if it were an oracle: "Whoever with skill and wisdom expertly asks, to him it will speak and teach him all manner of things." This relationship between music and prophecy is echoed in the Bible. When Jehoshaphat asked Elisha for an oracle, the prophet asked for a minstrel; when the minstrel played, Elisha began to prophesy. These cross-cultural similarities suggest an archetypal connection between music, Hermes, and prophecy.

We can think of prophecy as the art of finding out something that is unknown. Whether it helps a Taoist find the direction of Nature's flow, a prophet find the will of God, or a shaman find someone who has gone astray in the tundra, divination provides access to information that was previously unattainable.

When Elaine sat at the piano to play, her childhood dream was far from her thoughts, and her life myth was not yet known. Then music snuck, like a thief in the night, past all her conscious barriers and into the depths of her psyche. It brought back booty from those hidden places, information that she could use to make her life more meaningful and fun. Music, like Hermes, rose up to Heaven to laugh at the cosmic joke, stole into the Underworld to commune with the mummies, and came back to Earth to share its treasures.

Producing harmony from a tortoise was not Hermes' only musical inspiration. According to the *Homeric Hymns,* he also created the "resounding pipes which can be heard from afar." It is curious that Hermes is linked to both the lyre and the pipes, because these two instruments were diametrically opposed in ancient Greece. Apollo, the intellectual god of light, played the lyre, an instrument of order and harmony. The pipes, which were used as accompaniments to many a Bacchic orgy, were played by Pan, the instinctual god of the forests, as well as Dionysus and his companions in drunken revelry, the satyrs. There can be no greater contrast than between the austere sun god and those rabble-rousers.

Yet Hermes, who crosses all boundaries, bridged the chasm between them. He sits simultaneously on both sides of that fence, just as he is equally at home on Earth, on Olympus, or in Hades. To Hermes, what is the difference between meditation and passion, death and life, Heaven and Earth, dream and reality, self-discovery and art? To him, borders are places to meet, trade, communicate, and cross over; they are not fixed and impenetrable but rather moveable and porous. Hermes is the archetypal edge crosser.

The border crosser, the transformer, the messenger, the trickster. Yes, indeed, the trickster. Who else would make our voices crack, twist our fingers when we play, grab our instruments in mid-measure? Who else would spill paint on our canvas, give us writer's block, make us forget our lines, trip our feet as we make an otherwise graceful turn? The irrepressible god surely smiles when we value these supposedly improper things and follow him across the borders of our identities and into the unknown.

Try This:

1. Stand up. (It is important to stand for this exercise.)

2. Sing or play something, anything. (Even if you are not a singer or musician. Even if you are a painter or dancer who is reading this book for ideas about your special brand of creativity. Even if you have no creative identity yet. Just try it first with music. Later you can translate this exercise to any medium.) It doesn't matter what music you try to make, because you are going to pay attention to exactly what you are *not* trying to do.

3. Listen for the sound/music you don't mean to make—the unwanted or unintentional part, the part of the music you wish would not have happened. Keep playing until you notice something. But the moment you notice something, even something tiny or seemingly insignificant, pay attention to the quality of that unintentional music. Is it louder than you wanted? Softer? Hoarser? Faster?

4. Play or sing the same music as before, but exaggerate that unwanted quality. Keep exaggerating until it becomes almost absurd.

5. Now drop the original music and just play or sing or make sounds with that unintentional quality. After a while, let yourself also move (or change your body posture) in a way that goes along with that "music." Let your facial expression change to go along with that as well.

6. Imagine someone or something from a myth or fairy tale who would look, move, and sound like this. Maybe it is a

person (or a creature, or a being, or thing) from a story you already know. Maybe you can make up a story as you make the sounds, movements, and facial expressions. Don't stop to think about it. Let the figure and the story come from the experience itself. It is really important that this person/thing is not you, and that the story you remember or create has nothing to do with you or your life. Let it be like a myth or fairy tale—as impersonal and as strange as it needs to be.

7. Tell that story from the perspective of the person/creature/ being/thing that you have become. What is "your" history? You might want to write it down, maybe even draw a picture of the figure you have become.

8. What do "you" want to do in the world? How would "your" life be different from the person who began this exercise? What would "you" want to teach that person? Write these things down so you don't forget them.

9. Have you ever dreamed about such a figure? Or about someone or something with a similar energy?

10. Go back to your normal self. Does the normal "you" object to this new "you"? Why not be this new way, or at least a bit like this, all the time?

11. Try to imagine being a bit like this—in your life, in relationships, in the world. How would this new way of being change your life? Find at least one thing that is good about being this way, one thing that this new being could teach you. Don't stop until you have found something positive about it.

Chapter 5

Or Is It Art?

Sunset Song/Almost Missed

I have spent my whole life looking west when the sun sets. How many evenings have I patiently watched the ball flatten as it falls, waiting for colors to paint the sky? Now I am on North Stradbroke Island (also called Minjerribah), off the east coast of Australia. I came here to work on this book and escape the Polish winter. It's gorgeous here. I was sad, though, to find that although I have a beautiful view of the ocean to the east, the view to the west from this side of the island is mostly blocked by hills. I can still see a bit of the sunset, but not the whole wonder, so I stopped trying.

Then one day, just before dusk, I happened to look out my window. Far, far in the east, the tips of clouds were a shining pink. Strange, I thought. The next day I made sure to be outside in the late afternoon. Long before the show had even started in the west, the eastern sky was awash in color. The hues were subtler than I was used to, more like pastels, but just as beautiful.

How could I have missed that my whole life? Oh, yes. My back was always turned. Half the world didn't interest me. I was always waiting for what I expected to see. My one-sided focus had closed my eyes to the miracle transpiring just over my shoulder.

I wonder how often I do that. I wonder how often we all do that. Just imagine the new musical possibilities when we start listening to the things we normally don't pay attention to. Don't intend to play. Don't expect to hear. Imagine the potential we could unleash just by noticing a few of the things we normally miss when we create. The moments when magic is trying to enter.

I watched the sunset this evening. Both of them. Finally, it was all over. East and west were clothed in gray. I turned to go home when a light caught my eye. I almost missed the rainbow-colored ring as the clouds passed under the moon.

A Song from the Heart: Music and Emotion

Music and emotion are like two sides of the same sky. Light from one makes the other colorful and rich. Unfortunately we sometimes forget about our feelings while playing. Maybe that's because of the amount of technique we need to play or sing "correctly." The problem intensifies when we're not in touch with our feelings in the first place, and so don't know which ones to express. Unintentional music can bring us closer to our emotions—or to whatever experiences are deep within us. When this happens, the music starts to glow.

Michael, a big, barrel-chested classical singer, came for one session while passing through Zurich on tour. He was thinking of changing voice teachers when he got home. His present coach was very technical, and he thought he might do better with one who taught him to sing from the heart. When he sang, I was struck by the smile on his face, but I kept it to myself for the moment. Michael said that he was disturbed by shortness of breath, running out of air too soon. I asked him to sing even longer before taking a breath, so we could investigate what happened when he ran out of air. This caused his voice to break a little at the end of the phrase. Amplifying this, his voice became softer and broke even more. He said it sounded like someone crying.

When he listened, he became very sad. Michael told me he suffered a lot from loneliness. He spent his life working, often on the road. He longed for a partner to share his success or his sorrows. I was touched that this big man was being so real and vulnerable with a stranger. I imagined him singing songs about those sad feelings and asked him what the song was about that he had sung for me. (It was in Italian, which I didn't understand.) Michael laughed softly and said it was about the pain of being alone.

I was surprised, since he had been smiling when he sang it. He told me he had been taught to sing with a smile, and now did it by force of habit. I encouraged him to sing the song once more, while feeling all of his feelings about loneliness and longing. This time, his emotions really came through. He even cried during part of the song, singing through his tears.

Finding a new singing teacher turned out to be an inner process as well as an outer one. Shortness of breath, which he usually thought of as a technical problem to be overcome, led him to discover his own deep pain. This helped him to drop his technique for a moment and sing from the heart. Of course, the point was not to cry during a performance. A true integration would be to express his deepest feelings and still retain his technique. I never saw Michael again. I can only wish that his new teacher was able to help him with this poignant process of integrating song and soul.

Monk's Red Sneakers: Getting Out of Musical Ruts

A common problem for musicians is getting into a fixed routine in which the same thing is played over and over, the same style of music with the same interpretation. One of the biggest challenges is to keep the music fresh and alive.

Work with unintentional music is the quickest way out of musical ruts. By focusing on the sound that is different from the rest, it helps musicians find new ways of playing. This is radical because it doesn't impose a new style or method on the musician; instead it notices what is new in the music that is already being played.

Sam, a good-humored, low-key professional in his forties, came to a seminar with his electric piano. He complained that he was always locked into the same musical pattern when he improvised. Then he started playing many long chords with no breaks between them. Always keeping at least a few fingers on the keys even when changing the position of others, he created a plaintive improvisation of uninterrupted sound. When he picked up a finger here and there to change a note, though, the keys clicked. This clicking made a rhythm of its own, in stark contrast to the non-rhythmic chords.

The incongruity of these rhythmic clicks sparked my curiosity. When I asked him to make the keys click on purpose, Sam replied, "That is the place that I am stuck. That sound. That rhythm. I just want to like . . . " Here he paused, lifting his hands in the air, and then continued, "I won't take my hands off the keys." I pointed out that his hands were already doing what he said he would not do; they were suspended in the air, off the keys. When Sam saw this, he laughed and agreed to play with the clicks.

In order to make the clicks louder, Sam experimented with lifting his hands very suddenly. He really enjoyed this and did it more frequently so as to create even more clicks. The rhythm became faster. As result of this new speed, Sam hit a "wrong" note. When I supported him to play more wrong notes, the music strayed even further from his normal way of playing. His first improvisation had been harmonically "correct," with all of the chords blending smoothly into one another. Now he was playing notes that were "out" or off-key. Sam made a face.

"It is hard to get behind the wrong notes," he said. "I have a whole value system that says 'go for the right notes, find the right notes.' So this is hard." With a little encouragement, though, he played even more "out." The music that evolved reminded us both of Thelonius Monk, the innovative jazz pianist who made playing "out" in. Sam told me that when first learning to play, he had listened to Monk a lot. Here was a role model who could play wrong notes and still be musical. With Monk in mind, Sam played again.

This improvisation was rhythmically exciting and harmonically complex. There were wrong notes and right notes and pauses and breaks in the sound. Sam said he had never played anything like it before and he liked the change. For some reason, he imagined someone playing this way in a bar while wearing red sneakers. It seemed that along with a new kind of music came a new friend who wanted to play along.

Sam had to pass through two edges—one rhythmic, the other harmonic—in order to break free of his habitual way of playing. His exclamation, "I won't take my hands off the keys," revealed the first edge. People on edges often say they *won't, can't, shouldn't,* or *don't want to* do things. The absurdity of his sentence, though—in light of his raised hands—helped him to pass through this mental obstacle. The next block arose when Sam could not "get behind" the wrong notes because of his value system. Edges are often sustained by values and belief systems. Sam's system limited his music, keeping him in a prescribed harmonic and melodic structure in which only certain "right" notes were allowed. Luckily, he remembered Thelonius Monk. Monk can be seen as a *figure over the edge,* someone capable of doing the un-doable and getting away with it. He was all Sam needed to trust that those wrong notes could be right.

All of the "new" ways of playing came organically out of Sam's "old" music. He didn't have to do anything other than exaggerate what he was already playing unintentionally. Many musical routines can be broken or expanded by realizing that *the seeds of change are already present in the music that seems to be old and boring*. The only rut is a lack of awareness of the new music that is trying to happen.

A Kid's Voice: Musical Technique

From here we move into more surprising territory. Musical technique arises naturally from working with the unintentional aspects of music. By "technique" I mean the skills and methods people use when playing an instrument or singing that facilitate or enhance the production of music. It can include the way a pianist holds her arms, the position of her hands, or the way she moves her fingers or sits on her bench. It can include the way a singer stands while singing, how open her throat is, how she breathes, how much air she exhales, or which part of her head or body is producing the tone. Music or voice teachers can teach all of these techniques. But they can also be learned in an utterly different way, simply by following the process of the person who is playing or singing.

This is surprising because technique is often thought of as correcting the bad habits into which a musician naturally falls. *Amplifying* bad habits and mistakes goes against the conventional wisdom that tries to erase these problems. As you'll see, though, technical skills and specific mechanical ways of playing music more efficiently and "correctly" can and do evolve organically from unintentional music.

Abby wanted to learn to sing but she was not a very serious student. She rarely practiced between lessons and sounded about the same as she had when she started studying with me a few months earlier. Here she was again, standing in front of me, fooling around during the warm-up exercises at the start of her lesson. Because she was making fun of the exercises, she made mistakes.

My first reaction was to scold her and tell her to be serious, but I decided instead to try to find out what was behind her mischief. On a hunch, I asked her how old she felt. "Eight," she said with a gleam in her eye and a lilt in her voice. That lilt gave me an idea.

I asked her to sing the exercise like an eight-year-old. When she did, there was a new lightness in her timbre, an airiness. I suggested that she not warm up but instead let the eight-year-old sing a song. She sang one that normally gave her a lot of trouble. (She could never hit the high notes.) The little kid, though, had changed Abby's technique dramatically. Whereas she had earlier tried to force the sound out, now she gently let it come out naturally. Before, she had choked on high notes. Now she lightly touched on them. Her throat had been constricted. Now it was open and relaxed. She usually stood rigidly. Now she had a bounce in her knees and held her head high.

Whenever I had asked her to sing or stand like that in earlier lessons, it had made no impression on her. All of my advice and teaching was useless. Yet when we followed her process, the technique emerged organically. And since it came from her, she was able to remember and use it later. She did not have to remember how she changed her throat and body posture. She just remembered being an eight-year-old, and the rest came naturally.

With a Baby's Hands

Abby's story is colored by the possibility that, being her voice teacher, I may have unconsciously encouraged her to sing "correctly." But following the process can, itself, reinvent and enhance musical technique. Here is an example in which a classical pianist discovered new ways to play the piano, an instrument I have never studied or even played.

When Christa played for me, I had the strangest impression. Although the piece was by Chopin, I felt like I was in India. The notes were sustained for so long that they sounded like they were coming from a drone in Indian music. Maybe it was the room we were in. Maybe it was the piano. We couldn't figure it out, but Christa was curious enough to experiment with that sound. In order to make the drone more prominent, she said, she would have to make the lowest note sustain longer. To do this, she hit that lowest key much harder than the rest. Then she got to an edge.

She thought that the melody should be stressed, not the bass note. Going into unfamiliar territory, she played the piece with the deepest notes emphasized. She realized that she had to change her technique, since she usually accented the thumb in the bass chord, not the pinkie. (The pinkie finger of the left hand has the job of striking the lowest note.) She had to change the balance of how she held her left hand; instead of emphasizing her thumb, she let her whole arm and hand fall evenly. She laughed as she played and said that it was actually a lot easier to play like this. It was more relaxed and balanced. The feeling of putting her hand down was like a baby putting its hand down, she said. She was shocked that it was so simple.

Extending this new technique to both hands, she played the entire piece. A rhythm that had been difficult became easy when played in this way. She laughed again and played another piece that had given her trouble. Again came the new feeling of balance, and the way of using her whole arm and putting her whole hand down on the keys, like a baby, made the piece easier and more comfortable to play. Effortless, she said.

Analysis of Musical Structure

To the layperson, music may sound like an almost random flow of notes, chords, and rhythms. But to the musician or music theorist, these elements have a rich structure that can be analyzed. Music—whether it is blues, hip-hop, rock, jazz, classical, or folk, whether it is Western or from anywhere else in the world—is *structured*.

In the discipline of musical analysis, music is studied in terms of its structure. Musical analysis is a way of simplifying the music so that all of the frills are taken out and just the skeleton is showing. It is a way to discover the larger movements underlying momentary changes in melody and harmony.

Sometimes very complicated pieces of music can be analyzed and found to have very simple structures. An analogy might be that of a person walking down a city street, stopping at different shop windows along the way. She looks here, crosses the street, then re-crosses and retraces her steps to a window she missed before. At first glance it might look like she is meandering in a random fashion. But if all of the little turns are overlooked, we can see that she is heading steadily north. We get the same kind of overview from musical analysis. This is usually done by looking at written music and breaking it down structurally and mathematically. As the following examples will show, you can also discover musical structure by unfolding unintentional music.

The Singing Analyst

Martin and I always worked in his apartment so that he could play his own grand piano. He usually buzzed the downstairs door open and greeted me at the top of the steps. On this particular afternoon, though, the building was open so I just walked in. The staircase echoed with music. Martin was playing a piece by Ravel and making sounds with his voice. He had never done that when he played for me, so I listened for a while. He was singing, but not the same notes that he was playing. I was fascinated. When our session started, I mentioned what I had heard. He was surprised. He had never realized that he sang while playing, and was happy to work on it.

First we worked on a passage that he had played for me once before. It was so complex that I had not been able to follow it too well. But when he sang along, I was able to follow the melody amid all the frills. He was playing all the embellishments but singing only a simple melody, and suddenly the whole thing made sense to me. He played the complicated passage again, emphasizing the simple melody not just in his singing, but also in his playing. The piece seemed, to both of our ears, to flow more and seemed easier to listen to and understand.

At another complicated part of the piece, he realized that he was singing a bass line, but not the same bass line as he was playing. Instead, his singing alternated between two notes. The actual bass line went "down down down down," but those two notes that he sang went "down up down up." They fit perfectly with the music. He realized there was a very simple structure beneath all of the complexity. This helped him to play the difficult fingering without a problem.

Martin told me he had studied theoretical musical analysis at the conservatory but had not gotten much out of it. Since our "analysis" came directly from his performance, he could funnel it right back where it came from and where it belonged. "What good does it do me on paper?" he said excitedly. "Now I can hear it and play it!"

The Jerky Teacher

I worked with Martin regularly during that time. He was a highly trained and talented professional musician who was passionate about life and also very open to experimenting and learning more about himself and his playing. The experience of unintentional music leading to a practical analysis of musical structure caught us both by surprise. We actually thought it was a fluke, until it happened again. A few months after his singing episode, Martin was having trouble with a piece he was working on. He said it sounded jerky in certain spots. When he played it for me, he also made a few mistakes.

We worked first on the "jerks," moments when the music did not seem to flow. We pinpointed one such part of the piece and I asked him to make the jerk even more noticeable. As Martin did it more deliberately—by slightly pausing before the notes and then rushing into them—he realized that this was a very important transition point in the music. Working on the next jerky spot, he found that it had a similar harmonic structure, with the same notes as the first one. When he really emphasized the jerk, he understood that this moment was also a transition point. We were both intrigued. He played these two parts a few times and told me that they were the two most important moments in the first movement of the piece.

Then we went on to the mistakes. Emphasizing a mistake he had made, he was shocked to recognize yet another transition point, and here again were the same exact notes that had been important in the other transitions. The next mistake also came at such a moment of shift. In fact, it turned out that each time Martin made a mistake, it was at a point when the music was changing from one mood to another or from one harmonic structure to another. And each time, the same notes were involved. We started to understand that there were certain similar moments of transition throughout the piece. Although the passages seemed to be unconnected, they were actually linked in the way they changed and transformed. This was getting even more interesting, but it still wasn't helping Martin with his playing.

He said that he had never consciously paid attention to these transitions. He had just gone along with them, being pulled back and forth each time the music changed directions. He realized that this was what gave the music its jerky sound. I suggested that instead of going along, he could focus on making the shifts happen. As he played the entire piece again, this time intentionally emphasizing the moments of transition, Martin felt that he was steering the music. He remembered an old teacher who, while Martin was playing, used to sit next to him at the piano and play certain chords strongly to steer the music. He had really liked that. It had always been difficult for Martin to steer music himself. Just now he had discovered that if he knew when the music changed direction, and consciously focused on those moments, steering became easier for him.

Until that day, his music teacher could steer music, but he could not. But those strange jerks and mistakes were pulling Martin, turning him, steering him so he could steer the music. Instead of marching in lockstep toward his idea of what music should sound like, he let the jerks lead the way. They pushed him into their pot, cooked him in their juices, and spat him out the other side a changed man. The next time we met, a very happy Martin told me he had been able to steer all the pieces he had played that week. He had become the music teacher he was sure he could never be.

Almost Missed (Short Reprise)

I was walking on the beach last night. Lights from fishing boats shone like campfires dancing on the sea. My neck was sore from looking at the stars. Then clouds came and took away my pleasure. Turning to go home, I happened to look down for a moment. There they were. The stars were at my feet. Little blue lights glowing in the wet sand all around me. I heard later they were organisms in the midst of chemical reaction. To me they looked like tiny little living stars washed in by the sea. Just like Heaven on Earth.

Almost missed. I just wasn't paying attention. I thanked the clouds for disturbing my intention.

I wonder what else I'm missing. Maybe I should look over my shoulder right now.

Try This:

(Until step 6, this exercise is the same as the one in the last chapter. Then it moves into music and creativity.)

1. Stand up.

2. Sing or play something, anything.

3. Listen for something unexpected, something you don't normally pay attention to, something you don't intend to play. Keep playing until you notice something. But the moment you notice something, even something tiny or seemingly insignificant, pay attention to the *quality* of that unintentional music.

4. Play or sing the same music as before, but exaggerate that unexpected quality. Keep exaggerating until it becomes almost absurd.

5. Now drop the original music and just play or sing or make sounds with that unintentional quality. After a while, let yourself also move (or change your body posture) in a way that goes along with that "music." Let your facial expression change to go along with that as well.

6. Continue with those movements, that facial expression, and that body posture. And especially continue with those sounds and that music. Feel the energy behind it. Now identify fully with that energy.

7. How would this new energy like to make music? What would "it" want to create? Go ahead and let "it" do that. Let

this new energy sing, play, or create whatever "it" wants. Give "it" free rein for the moment, without judgment.

8. How is this different from your normal music or creativity? Is there something you like about it? Some new quality or energy? Try bringing this quality or energy into the music you originally played or sang. How does this change your playing? How does it change the music? Now let it create totally new music, if "it" wants to do that.

9. Does this new energy and quality have a different technique from what you normally use? Does it understand the music or art in a different way?

10. Be aware that new and unexpected things may pop up as you are playing, singing, or creating. Keep "looking over your shoulder" and let it unfold however it wants to unfold.

Part III

"Practice. Practice."

An old joke:
A famous violinist was on his way to give a concert at
Carnegie Hall, but got lost somehow. He stopped an aged
man on the street and asked, "How do you get to
Carnegie Hall?" The man looked at the musician, looked
at his violin and answered, "Practice. Practice."

Chapter 6

A Debate

Two voices are fighting in my head. One says that openness and curiosity about the unknown are all you need in order to play and work with unintentional music. He laughs at methods. He complains that the reason I got into so much trouble with my singing in the first place was that I got too caught up in trying to do it right. He says that if I had just followed my own natural way of singing, everything would have been better. He worries that if I try to teach you how to work with unintentional music—in other words, if I try to teach you the way I work with it—then I will send you down the same dead-end street I have finally found my way out of.

The other voice says that certain things are important to learn. He says that knowing some theory and methods can help you to follow the process. Otherwise, you may end up following the primary process or, even worse, pushing yourself or someone else into places that could be hurtful, both musically and personally. He says that the ancient Taoists studied themselves and studied Nature for many years in order to know the direction of the Tao's flow. In order to play guitar, he continues, it's easier to learn some chords instead of trying to figure out the whole thing from scratch. It makes sense to learn a few basics in order to work and play with unintentional music.

A third part of me sits above this debate and smiles. He is thinking of the old joke of a rabbi who was asked to solve an argument. One man told his side of the story. The rabbi listened and said, "You're right." When the other man explained his perspective, the rabbi said, "You're right." A bystander complained, "You said he was right and he was right. Certainly they both can't be right." The rabbi turned to him and said, "You're right, too."

There is not one correct way. Some people learn by having clear instructions and guidelines to follow. Others learn by trial and error. Some like the clarity of mathematical formulations. Others prefer feeling their way in a mystical darkness. I personally believe both sides are important. If you lose touch with your metaskills, your work with unintentional music may become a mechanical exercise. But if you don't have some basic skills, you may end up swimming around and not knowing what to do.

I spent years teaching seminars in which I explained about exact listening and neutral description. But students told me that when I worked, I didn't always follow my own recommendations. At first I thought I should try harder. Then I realized that perhaps something new was trying to emerge. That's when I started thinking more about metaskills and the importance of just following. On the other hand, if I had not spent those years being precise, I may not have known what to follow.

Many years ago, I had the great fortune to study with Bobby McFerrin, the wonderful jazz singer. I had seen a report about him on the local TV station in San Francisco. I fell in love with how freely he improvised. The next day, I was at an outdoor concert by the singer Taj Mahal and there was Bobby, standing next to me! I asked if he gave lessons. He smiled and gave me his phone number. Then he disappeared. Five minutes later he was on stage singing with Taj Mahal.

When I showed up for my first lesson I was ready to learn about freedom. But Bobby had something else in mind. He asked me to improvise within very specific structures. I couldn't do it, so he told me to study music theory and ear training and come back in six months. Man, was I disappointed. But I went off and studied hard. In our next lesson, I could do everything he had asked me to do before, but he gave me other tasks that were way beyond my knowledge and ability. So he told me to go to a certain teacher and study jazz theory and improvisation. Later, there were new challenges and new recommendations. I had come for freedom, but Bobby was teaching me about structure.

I always told that story as a way to prove to my students that they need to study the methods before they can work with unintentional music. But I always left out one part of the story. All of that studying did not help me to improvise. Many years later, though, I am really glad to have that knowledge. When I get an idea for a song, or there's a melody I need to find chords for, it is incredibly useful to have those resources inside me so I can midwife my inspiration and make it real.

The most important learning that I received from Bobby did not happen in our lessons, or in the hours, months, and years I spent studying between lessons. What most impressed me were the moments when we met on the street or in a cafe or took a long walk together. I was so touched by his humanity, his humility, his gentleness, his spirituality. I guess I would say that his metaskills were extraordinary and made a profound impact on me that lasts to this day. For me, those qualities are what make him such an amazing singer. On the other hand, without all of his incredible theoretical knowledge, experience, and practice . . .

The debate continues. It's probably best to offer you both options and to let you decide for yourself. You've already read the metaskills chapter. Following yourself and your music with curiosity, love, and awareness is one side of the coin. The other side will be presented in these next two chapters. But don't forget that the side you do not choose may be secondary for you. That means that if you decide to follow your own path, you may have an edge to study and learn. If, though, you choose to follow my instructions carefully, something deep inside you may be yearning to break free and follow yourself. Only you can know what is right for you. But do you know who in you is making the decision?

In case you're interested, here are some ideas that have helped me a lot over the years.

Try This:

1. Ask yourself where you stand in this debate. When you try something new, do you tend to value openness, curiosity, and experimentation? Or do you tend to feel that study and practice are more important? Even if you share both views, toward which side do you usually lean?

2. Take your own side. Why is this important to you? Write down a few key points.

3. Imagine yourself going even further in this direction. If you really did this more, took this point of view more seriously, what good effect would it have on your music or creativity? (If you really practiced, or really experimented, or whatever that side means to you.)

4. Find the other point of view inside of you. Imagine really embracing that.

5. What good effects would that have on your music or creativity?

6. Now do both!

Chapter 7

Listening to the Bare Bones of Music

Musicians around the world have told me that the most important part of making music is listening. It is also probably the most important skill when working with unintentional music. Hmm ... A dog is barking outside my window in staccato bursts. The wind is howling a long, unbroken, high-pitched melody. The door is knocking loosely against its frame, again and again and again. Computer keys are tapping away in quick, rhythmic clicks, interrupted now and then by long pauses. Evening improvisation for mixed sound quartet. Yes, hearing every sound as music is a first, vital step. Where do we go from there?

Neutral Language vs. Interpretive or Value-Laden Language

I often ask seminar participants to describe what they hear when someone sings or speaks. Many use words like "tight" or "sad" or "excited" or "strong." These words do not describe the sounds themselves, but are *interpretations* of the emotional or physical state of the person making the sounds. Once an interpretation is made, it is tempting to think we know everything about the sound, and about the person making it. We no longer hear the sound itself, but instead focus on the state that it is *assumed* to express. This can severely limit our ability to work with what people are actually playing and singing.

Some words used to characterize sounds are *value laden* as well as interpretive. When someone says that a voice sounds tight, there is often an underlying judgment revealing a belief that voices should be loose and relaxed. People in seminars commonly describe singing as stressed, uptight, tired, and choked. Such words carry with them negative connotations that create an atmosphere of denigration and failure instead of support and encouragement. Someone whose voice has been described as tight or tired almost invariably feels attacked and bad about sounding this way. She tries to change by relaxing or pepping up. That's fine if our goal is to attain some ideal of vocal production or to change people into an ideal image of how we think they should be. But our goal is to support and find the wisdom in what is naturally happening. Judgmental or value-laden words inevitably scare away unintentional music.

Auditory Subchannels

We need a neutral language for process work, one that is free of interpretation and value judgment. In order to listen and describe with as much openness and precision as possible, I find it helpful to think of sound in terms of its most basic components. I call these basic components "subchannels." They are the raw materials of sound and music. The auditory subchannels are:

Volume: The loudness or quietness of a sound or note.

Pitch: The highness or lowness of a sound or note. When a police siren goes up and down, it is the pitch that changes. The keys on the right side of a piano keyboard have a higher pitch than those on the left.

Timbre: The quality of a sound that distinguishes it from other sounds of the same pitch and volume. Imagine Luciano Pavarotti and Louis Armstrong singing the same song. For a more direct experience, start speaking aloud and then hold your nose while you continue speaking. The change you hear is a change in timbre.

Time: Includes how fast or slow the music or sound is (tempo), and the differences in duration of particular sounds or notes (rhythm). If you play a song on a tape player, and then speed up the tape, the rhythm of the music stays the same but the tempo gets faster. If, though, you play a blues and a waltz at the same tempo or speed—each beat takes one second, for instance—the rhythms of the two kinds of music are still different.

These subchannels can be combined. In this way, practically all music can be described by using just the four terms defined above.

Melody can be described as a succession of different pitches over time.

Harmony/discord can be described as consisting of two or more notes that are played or sung at the same time.

Dynamic can be described as the relationship of different volumes over time.

Subchannels help us to listen to just the bare bones of the music, before our thoughts, feelings, fantasies, interpretations, and judgments put "meat" on those bones. It brings us back to the most essential, basic level of what we hear. To find out why this is important, let's think about someone who "sounds sad" when she speaks.

Speech that is often interpreted as being sad can be described as having low volume, slow tempo with many pauses, and a relatively low pitch. A person who speaks this way may, in fact, be sad. But many different states could also be connected with those sounds. For instance, someone in a deep meditative state might very well pause a lot and speak slowly and quietly with a low-pitched voice. She could just as easily be thoughtful or confused or tired or in a trance, or trying not to show her anger. By labeling her voice "sad," we discount other possible meanings of those low tones and pauses.

By using a more precise and neutral description, we can support the person to discover for herself what is behind those signals. We could ask her to make the pauses longer, the volume lower, and the pitch deeper. Then she could go more fully and consciously into her experience. Maybe she would, indeed, discover sadness. But then we would be *working* with the sadness in her voice—letting the sound itself give her its message—not just reporting our idea about it.

The same is true when we listen to any kind of music. Describing what we actually hear, instead of interpreting and judging what we hear, is—in my experience—essential if we want unintentional music to tell us its secrets. It is equally necessary when you are unfolding your own unintentional music. Assuming that you know why you are making a certain sound, or that you know what process is behind it, is the surest way to stay within your normal manner of thinking about yourself and your music.

Subchannels As Continua

Subchannels can mostly be broken down into simple continua—continuous lines that stretch from one pole to another: Pitch is either higher or lower, volume is louder or quieter, pauses last a longer or shorter amount of time, and tempo varies from faster to slower. This makes it easy to think and talk about what we hear (see chart 4).

PITCH
LOWER ◄ - - - - ► HIGHER

VOLUME
QUIETER ◄ - - - - ► LOUDER

TIME
SLOWER/LONGER ◄ - - - - ► FASTER/SHORTER

Chart 4. This chart shows how sound and music can be described in terms of auditory subchannels. Each subchannel is a continuum between two poles. A specific pitch lies somewhere on the continuous line between higher and lower, for example. Awareness of this simple structure makes it easy to describe what we hear.

The Problem with Timbre

The one subchannel that is not based on a simple continuum is timbre. We have many names for different variations of timbre, some of which lie along their own continua. For instance, people speak of sounds as being hot or cool, rough or smooth, round or thin. Perhaps timbre could be incompletely portrayed by the following diagram (see chart 5).

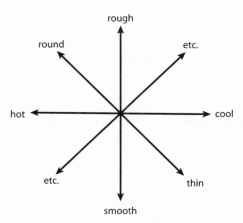

Chart 5. Timbre (the quality of a sound) cannot be depicted with one continuum. This chart shows some of the many continua that make up timbre.

The difficulty in describing timbre is compounded by the values placed on some of these words. For instance, rough and smooth have certain connotations in our society, as do cool and hot. Round and thin are visual descriptions of auditory phenomena and so may not be particularly useful. Timbre on the whole is a complex and rich phenomenon that is difficult to describe in a neutral and noninterpretive way.

As a result, when talking about a musician's timbre I often use a "blank access" statement such as, "There is something interesting in the tone of your voice." This sentence is so open that it allows the other person to fill in the blank about what I really mean by that. She can then listen to her timbre and hear for herself what might be interesting there. Another way to get around the timbre problem is to try to imitate the timbre that you hear. This kind of echoing is often more useful than describing the timbre by using a possibly interpretive term.

From Structure to Freedom

What has been outlined here is an almost mathematical representation of auditory phenomena. Sounds and processes, though, do not always fit into such neat schemes. (For instance, subchannels do not describe the difference between "ooo" and "aaa," or the many variations of "aaa" depending on language and accent.) So employ these ideas when they are helpful; when they outlive their usefulness, try something else. But don't forget to be as *neutral* and *noninterpretive* as possible.

Some people have an aversion to dry, scientific analysis. It can surely never represent the true Tao. It is also not very interesting to read such neutral descriptions in story after story. That is why I have used more colorful, less neutral language when relating the examples in this book. When actually working with people, though, I make every effort to listen, think, and speak as neutrally as possible.

The next chapter will show you how to use these ideas to work with your own unintentional music. Like the horn player who works on her chops in order to improvise better, or the classical musician who practices scales in order to better play Beethoven, let's take this structure and use it in the service of freedom.

Try This:

(You can do this exercise with a friend, or alone using a tape recorder.)

1. Say a single sentence.

2. Then say the same sentence, trying to alter one component, while keeping all the others constant. For instance, speak with a higher-pitched voice but do not alter the speed, timbre, or volume of your voice.

3. Your friend (or the tape recorder, when you play it back) can tell you whether you were successful. Your friend (or you) can try to figure out which subchannel you were trying to change, and which one was changing unintentionally.

4. Repeat steps 1-3 with different sentences.

Tip:

The point is not to be able to do it without a mistake (it's not as easy as it sounds), but to train you to listen to the different auditory subchannels in speech. This will also start to train you to notice unintentional music.

Chapter 8

Supporting the Insupportable: A Method to This Madness

Someone who says she learns from her mistakes usually means that she learns how not to repeat them. How much more creative it would be to really *learn from our mistakes by repeating them until we discover what was wise about them in the first place.* In jazz, there is an adage that if you hit a wrong note once, it is a mistake; if you hit it twice or three times, it becomes hip. Those old jazz players knew what they were talking about. Unintentional music can teach us things far beyond what we would expect. Before finding out how to coax it to give up some of its crazy wisdom, let's think for a moment about what unintentional music actually is.

A Message from the Unknown

Life is full of communication, not just when we talk to someone or write a letter, but all around us and inside us. When the phone rings and I don't pick it up, I am communicating that I don't want to be disturbed. When you have the flu, your body is communicating to you that you should rest. Everything we perceive is a communication or a potential communication. Aboriginal Australians, for instance, believe that when they look at a tree, that tree is communicating with them. Modern physics also tells us that there is a relationship between the perceiver and the perceived. Contrary to what we normally think, perception is not a one-way street.

Music is communication. Between performer and audience. Between composer and musician. Between the music and the feelings it stirs in you. Between your feelings and the sounds that are affected by them. Some people believe that music comes from God, or a spirit, or a muse. Or that music goes back out into the universe where it came from in the first place. It is hard to say from whom it comes and to whom it goes; but it is definitely communication.

Communication means there is a message. Often the message is clear. When Billie Holiday sang a sad song, full of pathos and pain, her message and the message of the music were the same. At other times, two messages may come out side by side. You may be singing a happy song, but feeling very sad. Maybe your voice breaks, revealing to all the world for that split second the true nature of your feelings, until you gather yourself together and continue your performance.

Those moments are so difficult. So embarrassing and annoying. They happen throughout life, not just when playing music. Have you ever had to act nice to someone you are furious at, smiling through your clenched teeth? Two messages—intended and unintended—compete for attention. You may know why your teeth are clenched, but not all unintended messages are so easy to understand. That's partially because messages do not appear in all their glory, ready to be received. They come out in little bits that are called signals.

If you sing that happy song, the break in your voice is a signal, just a small part of the message proclaiming your sadness. If the message would come out fully, perhaps you would cry or howl. But you may not want to do that. You may not even realize how sad you are. So a tiny crack in your voice sneaks out against your will. We can call the signals we don't mean to send "double signals" because they come out at the same time as the signals we do mean to send. Double signals help us to become aware of things we usually ignore, repress, or just do not notice. That's because those signals come from our secondary process, which is beyond our awareness and control. The unintentional parts of our music are double signals, tiny bits of messages from the unknown.

Unintentional music is a sign that the dreaming process is trying to lead us and our music in a certain direction. The trouble is, the message is not yet clear. It is like a weak signal on a radio; to know what song is playing, we have to turn up the volume. In order to know what our unintentional music is trying to tell us, we have to amplify the double signal.

Feedback

It's tempting, but misleading, to think that we already understand the message even before it has had a chance to express itself completely. It's equally tempting to think that we know the right way to amplify a signal, or even the right signal to amplify. In the following discussion of techniques that are sometimes helpful when working with unintentional music, please remember that no one method will always work. An acorn needs earth, water, and sunshine to grow into an oak tree; but a baby would not reach adulthood with the same nourishment. A tool that supports a certain signal once may not work with a similar signal in the next moment or with the next person.

The only way you can know whether you are doing the right thing is to check the musician's feedback. If she likes your intervention, do it more. If she smiles or immediately does what you recommend, well done. If she frowns menacingly, or shouts "No way!" you might also be on a good track, but an edgy one. If she ignores you, though, or just shrugs, or hesitates but then nicely goes along with your suggestion, you are probably striking dirt rather than gold. There's nothing bad about that. Just try again. Negative feedback can be very helpful. It is like a street sign that shows you are going in the wrong direction. Be thankful that you know it is time to turn around.

The same goes when you are unfolding your own unintentional music. Pay attention to your own feedback. If a part of you screams "No!" it may mean the path is wrong, or that the path is all-too-right but difficult. If your heart starts beating faster, or you get scared, those could be indications that you are going in a good direction. If the whole thing starts to bore you, try to remember the last exciting moment and go back to it. You might have missed an edge there. It is difficult to work alone, but not impossible. It just requires more awareness, discipline, and detachment.

Whatever you do, don't try to push yourself or another musician to change. *Change happens when it is trying to happen anyway.* Pushing and getting attached to your ideas will only make you feel frustrated, impatient, and annoyed with yourself or the person you are working with. The process is the wise one, not you. Let go of your concepts and trust what is happening. As Lao Tsu says:

> *The master sees things as they are,*
> *without trying to change them.*
> *She lets them go their own way,*
> *and resides in the center of the circle.*

With that in mind, here are just some of the myriad possible ways of supporting those parts of music that we normally think of as insupportable. Please use them as starting points in your own discovery process.

Exaggerating the Double Signal

The most common way to amplify a double signal is to exaggerate it. Isolating the signal's subchannel makes this easy. If a note is flat (or lower in pitch than it should be), play it even lower. If a tone is raspy when it was intended to be smooth, make it even raspier.

While participating in a seminar focused on group dynamics, I was asked by the facilitator to do a musical exercise with this group of about seventy people. I had them all sing a scale (do, re, me . . .) together and tell me what they heard. Quite a few people noticed that the very beginning of each note was much louder than the otherwise soft singing, so I asked the group to make a loud sound and then be quiet. No one was prepared for what happened next.

An amazing roar, a deafening cacophony of sounds was unleashed, and then just as suddenly, there was total silence. For five minutes you could hear a pin drop in this room crowded full of people. The mood had changed drastically. Many people felt a sense of oneness and connection in the silence that they had not felt before. Some participants described the thunderous clamor as making room for the silence or opening a hole in the space that made it possible for the silence to exist.

In the discussion that followed, it became clear that there was a polarization in the group between two opposing factions: One wanted peace and harmony; the other felt that harmony could only arise if they were allowed to fully express and process the conflicts that were present. Since this simple exercise was structured in response to the participants' own signals, it brought to the surface the as yet unspoken, underlying process of the group.

Any group can try this. Let the whole group sing something simple together. (A musical scale, "Happy Birthday," or a children's song that everyone knows would all work well.) Listen for what seems unintentional. Using the subchannel of the double signal (in our example, volume), ask the group to exaggerate that aspect of the music. This is likely to access the dreaming process of the group as a whole. Then you can either use whatever happens to make more music together, or talk about how the background process affects your life together.

Forbidding the Double Signal

You can also amplify a signal by forbidding it. Make a flat note a little higher so that it is no longer flat, or make a pause disappear. The idea is that by forbidding the signal, the impetus for it will become stronger. It is like using your thumb to stop a slow stream of water from coming out of a hose. Eventually the pressure will build up and you will be unable to hold it back any longer.

Magda's playing was filled with short pauses. When I pointed this out, she did not believe me and said that she liked playing the piece very quickly. Following her primary intention and forbidding the double signal, I encouraged her to play it even faster and under no circumstance make a single pause. Magda was happy with this suggestion. She looked like a tiger ready to pounce on the piano keys. When she played, though, Magda herself realized that she could not get far without pausing. I encouraged her to try it again but the same thing happened. She then became interested in investigating the pauses. By trying to stop the river, she became aware of the direction it was pulling her.

Making the Signal Happen More Often

A third possibility is to make the signal happen more often within its subchannel. Rather than working with a single pause, more pauses can be scattered throughout the music. Instead of having one note off-key, the entire piece can be played off-key. If there is a nasal quality to your voice on a single note, the entire song can be sung with that timbre.

Sara made sure everyone knew she was not a piano player. We were at the apartment of a mutual friend who had arranged an informal class as I was passing through town. There was a cozy atmosphere with everyone drinking tea as we talked about unintentional music. An old, rickety piano leaned against the wall. Sara had been eyeing it for a while. She was incredibly shy to play in front of us but also excited to try. She told us many times that she had not touched a piano for ten years and that she only knew one piece. Then she nervously sat on the piano bench and started playing.

Everything was going well. She not only remembered the notes but actually played with a lot of sensitivity. At one point, though, she paused for a short moment and then went on. Although it was "normal" to pause during the first run-through of a piece she had not played for ten years, I heard that signal as being potentially meaningful and suggested that she make lots of pauses throughout the music. She began to play very slowly. Then she hit a wrong note. Using the same intervention, I asked her to make more wrong notes.

To my surprise, she started to improvise. One of the notes was dissonant. I encouraged her to play other dissonant notes. The music became more and more far-out, both melodically and harmonically, but it was still very rigid rhythmically, each note being played for the exact same amount of time. Then one note made no sound at all when she pressed the key. (It was an old piano and she had not pressed hard enough.) I recommended adding more notes that did not make any sound. The music became really interesting. There were what seemed like random notes that were played very softly and others that had no sound at all. There were long pauses and then a soft note hanging in the air surrounded by more silence.

She said that in her mind's eye she saw a picture of water with the moon reflected in it and little pieces of wood floating on the water. Sara played on for a while and then said that she did not know why she was not scared. She thought that any normal person would be scared by this. I did not understand and asked her to explain. She had read of someone whose boat had been destroyed by whales. The person drifted in a raft for weeks before being rescued. She said that the music and the picture of the wood floating on water reminded her of this—that there were only small pieces of floating wood to hold on to in a big sea. But she felt strangely calm and not at all frightened like she thought she should be.

It came out that Sara thought of herself as a very organized person who plans her life around structured activities. She was usually frightened to go out of these set structures but said she was beginning to float a bit here and there. She was moved by the music and by her surprising calmness in the face of leaving the structures that normally organize her life.

The Flow Chart/Finding the Next Unintentional Signal

You may have noticed that each time Sara intentionally produced a signal that had been unintentional, another double signal occurred in a different subchannel. We can think about this in terms of Amy Mindell's idea of the "flow chart" that "maps the unique path that a process follows as it unfolds." The flow chart illustrates how a process that is initially secondary becomes primary as the person "picks it up" or does it intentionally. A new secondary process then arises, which the person may or may not pick up and make primary. Chart 6 maps Sara's process.

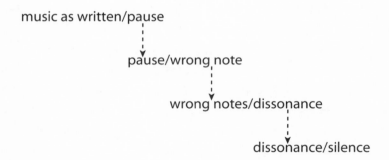

music as written/pause

pause/wrong note

wrong notes/dissonance

dissonance/silence

Chart 6. This "flow chart" shows how a process unfolds. Sara's original primary process (her original intention) was to play the music as written. A pause happened unintentionally; this was a secondary process. When she made more pauses *intentionally*, pausing became a primary process (because she was now intending to do it). Then another secondary process arose, an unintentional wrong note, which in turn became primary when she made wrong notes on purpose. Being aware of this progression of primary and secondary processes helps us to work with music by noticing and supporting the next unintentional signal.

We can see that the initial primary music (what Sara tried to play) was the piece as it was written. The pause was not deliberate. When this was called to her attention, she paused more on purpose. In this way, what had been secondary came under her control and became more primary. A new secondary sound arose, a wrong note. She took this over and intentionally made even more wrong notes. The improvisation that resulted was still very harmonic until the next unintentional signal came—a truly dissonant note. Once she deliberately played with dissonance, a double signal occurred in the volume when a note she had tried to play made no sound.

When all of these signals were integrated consciously into the music, the channel changed and she saw a picture. In each instance, a new unintentional signal arose after the last one had been "picked up" or played with deliberation and intent.

An awareness of the flip-flop nature of processes is a valuable tool. Noticing and encouraging each new aspect of unintentional music as it arises is an important way of unfolding the process. This method is similar to the work of sketch artists who make composite pictures of a suspected criminal. First they find the right kind of nose, then mouth, then eyebrows. Eventually they fill in the whole picture. Of course, our goal is to follow the process, not catch a crook (although Hermes, the thief, might be lurking in the darkness). By supporting each component of the music as it changes, we can fill out our unintentional music, helping it to complete itself and show its wisdom.

Channel Changes

Sara's process started musically, then changed to another channel when she saw a picture. The dreaming process flows through all channels, so it is useful to remember that any of your experiences could have a potentially meaningful relationship to your music. Of course, when playing, your attention and intention are focused on the music. Still, it can be exciting to notice what irrational things are taking place in other channels while you play.

Franz, a classical guitarist, put his hands over his face for a moment just before starting the piece. For some reason, his gesture stuck with me and I could not focus on the music, wondering why he had done that. When he finished playing, I wanted to ask him about it but was afraid that the answer would come from his normal identity. Instead, I thought it would be better to let the signal explain itself.

I asked Franz to put his hands over his face again, wait in that position for while, and then report his experience. He said that he was feeling his body, so I asked him to put down his guitar and go ahead and let himself do that. Franz said that he would be able to feel himself even better if he were lying down. He made himself comfortable on the floor and closed his eyes. After a while, his chin began to rise slightly, so I gently put a finger under it to support his awareness of this movement. His chin went up more and more until his back was arched. This continued, very slowly, until only his head and feet were touching the floor. Franz's body began shaking a bit, then more and more, faster and faster, in this arched position. He screamed with delight and exclaimed that he saw colors shooting out of his glands. It looked like he was enjoying himself immensely.

When he settled down, he said that he had seen an image of himself doing this on the Bahnhofstrasse. (We were in Zurich, Switzerland. Bahnhofstrasse is the city's most exclusive shopping street and the seat of Switzerland's largest banks.) Franz saw not only himself but everyone on the street going into a wild state with him. We talked about how this would be truly a secondary process for the whole city. (Zurich is certainly not known for its wild, public outbursts of expression.) He spoke excitedly of how he could bring this energy into his relationships.

Then I asked him whether he could express this ecstatic wildness in his music. Franz grabbed his guitar and played the same piece as before. But this time he played it with incredible energy and the same feeling he had had when colors were shooting out of his glands. He said, with an irrepressible smile, that he had never thought it was allowable to play like that.

By looking down and covering his eyes just before playing, Franz was unconsciously trying to get in touch with his feelings. As he allowed his process to develop, it led him through many channels. His feelings (proprioceptive) moved him (kinesthetic), made him see colors (visual), and made him make sounds (auditory). Then he saw himself (visual) doing this with other Swiss people on Bahnhofstrasse (world) and spontaneously fantasized about being this way with friends and lovers (relationship). All of these channel changes were organic, a part of the natural flow of his process. Following these changes helped him to immerse himself in the experience and to bring its ecstasy back into his music.

Channel changes don't have to happen organically. You can also change channels intentionally. Once you have accessed your unintentional music you can, for instance, imagine a picture or make a face or movement that goes along with the new music. This fills out your experience, making it more tangible. It also puts you in touch with the unknown part of you who is playing. But if you are changing channels on purpose, it's important to do it only after you have already gotten to something secondary in your music. Otherwise the picture, facial expression, or movement will be a translation of your intentions, which won't bring you or your music that freshness you were searching for.

Stories and Speech Echo the Music

When people come for sessions to work with their unintentional music, the primary focus is on the music. Outside of this focus is the casual conversation that happens before the work officially begins. People talk about how the day has been, the other aspects of their lives, their moods, and their relationships. Anything can come up in the time between entering the room and getting down to the business at hand. By listening carefully to what is said, it is possible to anticipate and work with the musical process that is about to unfold.

One important process work tool is the ability to analyze a person's speech in order to discover information about her process. The syntactic structure of speech, for instance, reveals which processes are primary and secondary. Simply put, if the speaker is also the "doer" in a sentence, then the action described is primary (for example, "I type"). If the doer is someone or something other than the speaker, then the action described is secondary (for example, "The monster tore the city apart"). This is a gross oversimplification of a complex and detailed theory. But, for the moment, it's enough to say that the actions and qualities associated with the speaker are primary, whereas those associated with other people or things (as well as those things that disturb "me") are secondary.

When you are equipped with this knowledge, the chat before a session becomes a rich mine of useful information. By analyzing what someone says, you can guess what kind of unintentional things may come out of, or need to be supported in, the music. I was lucky to be invited by a piano teacher to sit in on his lessons in order to help him incorporate process work into his teaching. Although music lessons will be addressed in depth in the next chapter, the following anecdote is a good illustration of the value of listening to what is said before any music is played.

Willie, who was ten, walked into the music room talking. He went on and on about his elementary teacher, who was sick a lot and missed school at least once a month. Then he said that he (Willie) wanted to practice piano all the time but that he had had a bad headache the day before, which had prevented him from playing. He talked for so long about how much he wanted to play that the lesson did not actually start for quite a while.

Looking only at what he said, it is clear that he was identified with wanting to play all the time. This was his intention. The teacher who was often sick, as well as the headache that disturbed his plans, were aspects of his secondary process. Interestingly, both the teacher and the headache had similar qualities: the teacher often missed work, and the headache stopped Willie from practicing. This process was mirrored in the lesson itself. Although he said he wanted to work, Willie talked so much that very little was actually done.

He then played very quickly and was distressed about the mistakes that held him up. But he still wanted to play fast. Trying again and again, he eventually got frustrated and could not play at all. Here was the same pattern of primarily working hard and doing a lot, and secondarily stopping and not being able to do anything. We spent the rest of the lesson chatting about the conflict between these two parts of himself. We did not "do" anything more that day. I had the feeling he needed a break anyway, and that the more we pushed, the more he would be stopped by his headache or his mistakes or something else.

We didn't work with the "not doing" either, since working was exactly what he had been doing too much of. He seemed to enjoy the vacation. The following week, Willie was able to have a normal lesson, with a more relaxed attitude about playing and working.

Dreaming into the Music

So far all of these interventions follow the principle that being as neutral as possible and following a musician's process allows unintentional music to unfold in its own natural way. I support that idea wholeheartedly. But it's not good to be too one-sided. Sometimes, when working with musicians, my own dreaming process gets interested and wants to play along. When I first started noticing this, I tried my best to repress it, convinced that the musician's process was more important. More and more, though, I trust that my dreaming, when it starts acting up, has something spicy to add to the soup.

Arthur, another classical guitarist who came to one of my seminars, looked like an intense man. His deep-set, icy-blue eyes seemed to eat up the world around him. He very much wanted to work on his music, and when his turn came, he played a piece very quickly. He said it was frantic and that he was pulled along by the music. Arthur complained that, although he tried to play correctly, he often got lost and hit the wrong notes. As I listened to Arthur play and talk, I had an irrational experience that I could not explain or justify.

I saw in my mind's eye a very big jazz guitarist whose hands dwarfed the neck of the guitar. He was drunk and just banged on the strings and did not care whether he played the right notes. I tried to focus on the music and on Arthur's problem, but this over-sized drunkard would not leave me alone. I finally stopped fighting it and told Arthur what I was seeing. He giggled. So I asked him to play as if he were this big, drunken jazzman.

Arthur played the same piece as before, but although the tempo was just as fast, it was not frantic. The music even seemed calm. He told me he had been able to express his feelings while playing instead of just being concerned about the notes. He said that that is how he likes to listen to music, while drinking wine and being content with what is happening in the moment and *feeling* his feelings. He was surprised he could have the same experience while playing. It did not hurt that when "drunk" he had made no mistakes.

Whether you are working with your own unintentional music or with another musician's, dreaming into music (or dreaming into the musician) can be very powerful. It is like letting the music (or musician) get into your pores, or inhaling it and letting it work on you. If you are working with someone else, check the feedback to make sure your fantasy or feeling is right for her.

Arthur giggled when I told him my fantasy and immediately wanted to try playing like a drunken jazzman. Another musician might have said that it was a stupid image or that it had nothing to do with her. Or she may have looked right through me as I related it, or waited for me to make another intervention, or fiddled with her instrument until I came up with something more applicable to her process. As always, if it is not useful to the person with whom you are working or if she does not pick up on it, there is not much to do besides dropping your idea and trying something else.

One person's thoughts and fantasies are normally not considered to be part of someone else's music. In the same way, what is said in passing before someone plays is normally considered to be outside the frame of the music. Process work constantly shifts the frame and helps us notice a connection between things that seem to be unrelated.

When I was a child growing up in the Bronx, New York, I used to play pool in the basement of my elementary school. I was never very good but it was a wonderful way to spend the afternoon. I remember one time looking at the table and literally seeing a web of roads connecting all the balls and all the pockets. I understood that I only had to hit the cue ball down a road, and it would hit the next ball at the correct angle and the ball would go in. It worked! One ball after another fell into the pockets. I had discovered that these seemingly separate entities were actually connected.

Unfortunately, I never managed to do this again at the pool table, but I have very often experienced it with music, dreams, poetry, and people. The things we think of as separate balls or unrelated factors are really somehow mysteriously connected. If we could just open our ears and eyes and hearts and minds enough to find out how they are connected.

Try This:

1. Sing any song.

2. Notice the unintentional part of what you are singing. It may be a slight mistake. One part of the song, or the whole song, could be louder or softer, higher or lower, faster or slower than you imagined it would be. Or maybe your tone of voice sounds weird to you. Or maybe one part of your song does not quite go along with the rest of what you sing. It might just catch your attention, spark your curiosity, or surprise you. There might even be a disturbing sound from your environment, or a conflicting sound or song in your head.

3. Now describe that double signal to yourself in a neutral way. In what subchannel was it?

4. Exaggerate the unintentional part of your music by doing it even more in its own subchannel. For instance, if it was too fast, make it even faster. Sing this again and again, amplifying the double signal, letting it unfold in its own way.

5. Find the next unintentional signal and repeat steps two through four.

6. You might want to imagine someone or something who would sing this way, and how she, he, or it would influence your music and your life if given the chance.

7. What do you have against this new influence? Why not sing and live like this all the time? Who would not want you to? Your answers to these questions show your edge.

8.Could there possibly be something good about making music and/or living a little bit like this?

Metaskill Alert:

Don't forget to stay open and loving toward this new music and this new part of you that emerges. Otherwise it may crawl back into its hole and not come out again except to disturb your next song.

Think of the unintentional signal like a leaf on a stream, showing the direction of the flow. By nudging it in the same direction that it is already going, you become a part of the stream, helping the process to flow in its natural course.

Part IV

Variations on a Theme

Like a harp, any sound I make is music.

–Rumi

Chapter 9

Process Oriented Music Lessons

A friend of mine had hated violin lessons as a child and had done everything in her power to avoid them. She forgot her music, lost it on purpose, even grew her fingernails so she could not play. Sometimes she snuck into the practice room early and set the clock ahead so the lessons would be over sooner. This girl also used to study piano and wanted to continue, but her teacher liked violin better and made her switch to his favored instrument. Piano lessons had been no treat, either. Whenever she hit a wrong note, he hit her on the knuckles with a ruler.

A dancer I know has been terrified to sing ever since a teacher told her that she sounded horrible. She had always wanted to be in the chorus of musical comedies in high school, but never auditioned because of her early trauma. To this day, she loves music and mouths all the words to her favorite songs, but will not sing a note.

A professional violinist told me that, as a child, he had a teacher who used her bow as a sword. Whenever the boy's timbre was a little off, or when he played a wrong note or rhythm, the teacher swung her bow and hit him with it. She conducted with the bow as well, making quick jabs in the air, and he was never sure when it would strike next.

Other friends, colleagues, students, and clients have related similar experiences. When someone mentions one such horror story, it often sparks a chorus of, "Oh, yeah. That happened to me, too!" In fact, one friend who read this chapter in manuscript form wrote in the margin, "I used to have an orchestra conductor who'd throw his baton at me like a spear if I screwed up."

Of course, it is unfair and inaccurate to categorize all music lessons or music teachers in such frightful terms. I have been blessed with some amazing music teachers. They taught me to love and appreciate music and myself. Nevertheless, the fact that so many people report bad experiences emphasizes the importance of teaching music in a way that encourages the student's creativity and individuality. The ideas in this chapter are meant to supplement the good and important work that the huge majority of music teachers are doing. When a lesson feels more like a dentist appointment, process work's fresh approach may provide relief for teacher and student alike.

Problem Areas in Music Lessons

The problems encountered by music students and teachers can, I believe, be traced to certain core issues. One of them is the focus on learning to play "correctly." Although techniques are just means to an end, they are sometimes given priority over the music they allow us to play. The proverbial rap on the knuckles does not sting as deeply or have as lasting an effect as the experience of having your own newly emerging musical nature discouraged.

It is normal for teachers to think they know how music should be played, since they are experienced musicians whose job is to impart their knowledge. But they then run the risk of ignoring whatever different ideas or feelings their students may have about the music. It could be that an open-minded teacher may even learn something from a novice. If the student is treated from the start like a musician, then the lesson becomes a creative project for both parties. Of course, some things simply need to be taught. It is a question of attitude, of metaskills.

Other potential problems involve the relationship between student and teacher. Relationship issues are often not resolved or even addressed. This is partly due to a lack of tools. But, just as importantly, student and teacher may feel uncomfortable speaking directly about something so personal during the time that should be devoted to learning music. Yet differences of opinion, disputes, and rebellion can and do interfere with learning. Student and teacher sometimes secretly hate each other and dread the upcoming lesson. On the other hand, love may also take the focus off the music itself.

Power struggles are another common pitfall in music lessons, as they are in teaching in general. Yet this issue is rarely, if ever, dealt with directly. Instead, the teacher might tell the student what to do and the student, in order to feel her strength, rebels by not paying attention, not following instructions, or not practicing. Although the teacher may feel helpless in such a situation, she has more rank and privilege, especially if the student is a child. This inequality can be further magnified and reinforced if the parents side with the teacher. Sometimes the only way for the student to win the struggle is to stop playing altogether. But this is a sad solution for the child who is then cut off from making music, sometimes for a lifetime.

Process work provides insights and tools that help explain and alleviate these problems. By noticing and supporting unintentional music, loving the mistakes and unusual sounds that most teachers would want to erase, a process oriented music teacher can help students become musicians who value their own ways of playing. Working with the process of the student as well as the interaction between student and teacher can make it easier for music teachers to get their ideas across and can give the students power in an uneven hierarchical relationship—power that normally only disturbs the lesson but could be used to further it.

All of the examples in this chapter are the result of my work with one gifted piano teacher I'll call Rob. He was brave enough to invite me to sit in on his lessons so that together we could research ways of applying process work in this unique setting. I am eternally grateful for his openness, humility, and sense of adventure.

Amplifying the Mistakes

Music teachers naturally notice and correct musical mistakes made during a lesson. In extreme cases, they even chide the student for the error. More compassionate teachers will gently point out a mistake and suggest ways to remedy it. In either situation, the goal is to erase the mistake and get on with playing the piece correctly. As we have seen, though, merely correcting a mistake may ignore valuable secondary information contained in it. If the mistake is supported and amplified, the music may even improve.

Joseph seemed like a very serious thirteen-year-old, dressed in a shirt buttoned all the way to the top. He entered the music room of his school in Zurich, Switzerland, and shook Rob's hand. When I was introduced, he called me by the formal "Sie" even after I suggested that he use my first name. This surprised me because most Swiss kids I have met are thrilled when they are allowed to be informal with an adult in authority. Not Joseph. He just opened his school bag, which had various folders inside that organized his papers and books. Out of one of these he took a pile of sheet music and neatly set it on the corner of the piano. Rob had assigned him a new piece to practice at home, a blues piece. This was the first non-classical music he had ever attempted to play, and he seemed a bit embarrassed about it.

His rendition was pretty stiff, since he was playing exactly what was written on the page. Now, it is usually good to play the notes on the sheet music, but it's very hard to write down the rhythmic and melodic nuances of the blues. As a result, when Joseph was playing note for note, it just didn't sound right. Having sung the blues for years, I tried to explain and demonstrate how it should sound. I couldn't show him on the piano, but using my voice and body movements, I did my best to get across how he should play.

Joseph looked at me with vacant eyes and played the tune once again just as before. He made a mistake with the tempo, though, continually speeding up. One option here would have been to didactically teach him how to stay in tempo. Instead, Rob and I decided to explore whether his mistake could be useful, so we asked Joseph to play even faster. As the tempo increased, he started playing wrong notes, sliding from one note to another, from a black key to a white one. He hit himself on the leg for the mistake, but we praised him for it and encouraged him to make the same "mistake" again. This was starting to sound like the blues, with the "blue notes" sliding into the regular ones.

Then he made a mistake in the rhythm, pausing slightly after the first note of the bass line and rushing ahead after the second. Joseph was again upset about his error. But we supported this, too, encouraging him to pause even more and then rush even more, exactly where the mistakes were naturally happening. The rhythmic changes gave the music a "groove." It was starting to sound bluesy. Joseph started to smile and even sway a bit with the music. He said he was surprised that he was actually supposed to play something that was not written down. The thought had never occurred to him before. Joseph played again, excitedly experimenting with his newfound musical freedom. I was happy to hear a bit of soul injected into his music, and to see the smile on his previously somber face.

Rob told me later that he normally had a hard time teaching this piece because, being a classical pianist, he had no experience playing the blues and could not teach the feeling or the groove. But even with my blues background, I had not been able to help at the beginning either. I was sure that I knew how it should sound, but Joseph would not listen to my good advice. This can be frustrating for any teacher who wants to share years of experience and accumulated knowledge. Sometimes, though, the only way to learn is to follow what is happening. *The process itself, manifesting in the mistakes that he made, taught Joseph the blues.* (Probably all of us have made some mistakes in life that have taught us the blues!)

Teacher Knows Best?

Joseph ended up playing the way I thought the blues should be played. But the process does not always lead the student to play the way the teacher thinks is correct. In fact, one of the easiest ways of finding a secondary process in a lesson is to find out what the teacher does not like in the student's playing. This is because the teacher, as the identified leader and the one who says what should be done, is often the keeper of the primary process of the lesson. When the teacher notices the flow of the lesson going against her intentions, a conflict arises. Should *her* ideas or the *student's* musical process be followed?

This decision must be left up to the individual teacher. It may be difficult for her to let go of her ideas. Teachers sometimes get irritated with students and even feel that if a student does not play "correctly," then that means they are bad teachers. Their own inner critic, who establishes this equivalency between the student's performance and the teacher's worth, makes it even more important to them that the student plays the way the music "should" be played. But when a teacher has the courage to stop thinking that she knows best and trusts the student's own creative process, amazing things can happen.

During the discussion about Taoism in chapter 2, we touched on an interaction between a girl and her piano teacher. Let's take a closer look. In that hour, a nine-year-old named Barbara was supposed to play a series of short melodies from her lesson book that she had practiced at home. The very moment she completed one, Rob made a check in the book and bade her continue to the next. Barbara, on the other hand, took her time arranging her fingers on the keyboard, making certain that each finger was correctly positioned. During one of the melodies, she made a rhythmic mistake, pausing too long after one note. Rob played it correctly (without the pause) and asked her to imitate him and also quicken the tempo. Barbara responded by spending a very long time arranging her fingers, then lifting them off the keys and starting fresh with her positioning.

Realizing that she would not cooperate with her teacher's wish for speed, I encouraged Barbara to take as much time as she needed to begin, and then play as slowly as she wanted, allowing as many pauses as she wanted. She played the piece again. What had been a quick little ditty became a piece of unusual power and sensitivity. The depth of her emotion came through in her playing, and both Rob and I were dumbfounded. Neither of us could have guessed at the potential of either the music or the child. Rob realized that the carefulness of her fingering and the pauses in her playing actually hinted at a profound musical process. Rather than being a pain in the neck of a student, Barbara was a budding musician.

When teaching in India, I had the opportunity to spend some time with a master of the veena (a string instrument played in Indian classical music). Ustad Dagar said, "You cannot learn without teaching. I teach themes. The student makes a mistake and apologizes. But the teacher learns something new from that." His words ring true, showing that he is a master not only of his instrument but of life as well. As Barbara's mistakes transformed a cursory exercise into real music, Rob listened and learned from his youngest teacher.

Meta-Awareness: How the Interaction Echoes the Music

Students, even those with very little musical experience, can show something new to the most seasoned instructor. This does not mean that everything a student says should be heeded, but that her process has a wisdom all its own. Barbara's process did not happen in a vacuum, though. It was a part of a larger context that included Rob. Their interaction had its own structure, which was curiously similar to the structure of Barbara's musical process.

Rob had set the pace for the lesson by rushing through various exercises, making a mark in her book the moment a melody was completed, and urging her on to the next without a pause. Barbara broke this rhythm by pausing for a very long time before playing. Looking at their interaction as if it were a piece of music, the intentional tempo was fast (the primary process determined by the teacher), while the double signals came in the form of waiting between melodies as Barbara arranged her fingers. When she played, the intentional quickness was also interrupted by an unintentional pause. The same pattern was present in the relationship and the music.

This kind of meta-awareness (awareness that the same process occurs in different channels) is a useful tool. Noticing the interactional pattern of a lesson can help you to form a hypothesis about what will be secondary in the student's playing. Barbara and Rob's unspoken sparring about time brought my attention to the time subchannel, and I was not surprised to find the same pattern in the music. Once Barbara played slowly, the atmosphere in the room cleared up. There was no more conflict, no more power struggle, just three people united in their love of the music.

The Student-Teacher Relationship

Ruth, eleven years old, strode into the room, sat down on the piano bench, and instructed Rob, "Write down at the end of the lesson exactly what my homework is." This first sentence is already a gold mine. From it, we can guess that Ruth's primary process was to be a student who followed the teacher's instructions and needed to be told exactly what to do. The double signal was the way that she spoke to her teacher: Her "request" was stated in the form of a command.

Her secondary process was to be the one giving the orders, to be the teacher giving an assignment. We could say that she projected her own ability to be a teacher—one who tells others how and what to learn—onto Rob, who was the identified teacher. Although primarily she wanted to be told what to do, secondarily she knew exactly what she needed and told him how to give it to her. This, in a nutshell, is a picture of one aspect of her individual process. Let's continue.

Ruth played a difficult piece very quickly and made only a few mistakes. Rob complimented her, saying that she had played it well. But Ruth was not happy and complained about the mistakes. He offered to give her hints about how she could play it better, but she refused to listen to him, saying, "I want to play but I don't want to practice." At this point, Rob turned to me and complained that she was always like this and that he did not know what to do anymore.

Now let's examine Rob's process. He was identified with being a teacher; he offered tips about playing better, and told her how to practice. His double signal, however, was to turn to me and ask for help. Complaining to me was an attempt (probably

127

unconscious) to get me on his side, to make a coalition with me against Ruth. It showed that he felt weak in relation to her. Also, he looked to me for guidance, for instructions about what to do next. His secondary process was to be weak, to not know what to do, to be a student.

Flip-Flop Processes in a Field

We see that their primary and secondary processes were mirror images of one another. This kind of inverse process structure, in which one person's primary process is the other's secondary and visa versa, is a typical pattern in relationships.

Instead of looking at their individual processes, we could think of Ruth and Rob as a single unit. In that unit or field were two polarized roles: the teacher who knows and gives orders, and the student who does not know and takes orders. Rob or Ruth could have occupied either role, since both of them had both roles inside of them. But each person was identified with only one role, and the other side came out only in their double signals. This dynamic was frozen by their identities and by their assigned roles in the lesson. Since it was frozen, and since the conflict between the poles was happening without awareness, it interfered with their relationship. (She resisted and he became frustrated.)

Occupation Theory

In such a situation, it is useful to remember occupation theory. But first, remember the children's game, musical chairs. The players walk around a row of chairs and, when the music stops, everyone must sit in a chair. There is one chair less than the number of players, and the one without a chair has to drop out of the game. In occupation theory, the roles in a field can be thought of like the chairs in the game. The person sitting in a certain chair is occupying that role in the field. In our example, one chair would be the role of the teacher and the other would be that of the student. What is important to remember is that *the chair, not the individual, defines the role.*

That means that individuals can switch roles and are not stuck with the same one for an entire lifetime. Unlike the game of musical chairs, the point is not winning or losing but, rather, that all chairs (or roles) must be occupied at all times. This means that if someone is sitting in the chair that you normally sit in, you *must* sit in the empty chair. In other words, if one person switches roles, then the other is forced to switch as well.

Using this theory, I asked Rob to stop teaching for the rest of the lesson. My hope was that this would leave the "teacher's chair" empty, allowing Ruth to occupy it. At first it didn't work because he would not leave his role. He kept telling her how to practice, and she continued to resist by making faces and excuses.

Flipping the Process

I saw that Rob was stuck in his role, so I entered the system myself in order to flip it. I told him that I was his teacher and that he was forbidden to teach. I said that I did not care what *she* did, but that *he* was no longer allowed to teach. I usually don't intervene so strongly, but I did here in order to occupy the teacher's role more congruently than he had, so that he would be forced to leave it. Rob sat silently, clearly wondering what I was up to. I told Ruth that it did not matter to me whether she went home or fooled around or played or worked or did anything else she wanted. I then leaned back and started talking to Rob about something else. In this way, I left the teacher's role myself, so she did not have to resist me. With no one at all in that chair, I suspected that Ruth would fill it.

Ruth looked perturbed for a minute and then announced loudly that she thought she should practice the piece very slowly.

(Remember that she had played it very quickly at first, and had made a few mistakes.) She looked at Rob for confirmation but both he and I ignored her. After playing it slowly, she asked him what to do next. He said that he did not know. She said that she needed to change the fingering in one spot where it was difficult to play. She asked him if she was correct in her judgment and how to do it. He did not answer, and she changed the fingering by herself. (Rob later told me that she had changed it to the "correct" fingering, the one he had wanted to show her.)

After practicing for a while, she asked for a homework assignment. I told her she could do whatever she wanted, including *no* homework, or whatever. Ruth proceeded to tell us exactly what she should practice at home. Then she said that this homework would take only fifteen minutes and asked what else to do. In the ensuing silence, she took out her exercise book and found some other homework to do in addition. She wrote down all of the assignments that she had given herself and flourished it in front of us, beaming and smiling from ear to ear. Rob praised her and Ruth went home.

Although the lesson ended well and everyone was happy, I was not totally satisfied. The point was not only that Ruth become her own teacher, but that she become Rob's teacher, and he her student. The intervention did a good job of accessing her secondary process; she was a very capable teacher, able to discover on her own how to play, able to give her own assignments. But my intervention had inhibited the interaction between them, and so did not touch on the process of their relationship as a whole.

A New Way of Teaching

Like individuals, relationships have primary and secondary aspects. Looking at this relationship, we could say that its primary process was a traditional piano lesson in which the teacher tells the student what to do and how to do it. The relationship's secondary process was to find new ways of learning and teaching, in which the student becomes the teacher and teaches him how to teach.

In her first sentence, Ruth was already moving in this direction, telling Rob exactly what she expected of him as a teacher. If she would have gone further with this, she might have told him exactly how she needed to be taught. Her edge was to unfold her ideas of what she really needs; his was to give up his old teaching style and learn from her. The larger pattern in the background that was trying to come to the surface was the mutual development of a new way of teaching in which the teacher helps the student to bring out her own ideas and creativity.

The old teaching style is not the fault of this particular teacher. Rob is an especially open and loving man who welcomed me into his classroom exactly so he could learn new ways of teaching. He tries with all of his might to be fluid and helpful to his students. No, not the individual, but his background was the culprit here. Like most musicians, he was trained in an old-fashioned system that values discipline and demands that the powerless student pay homage to the teacher. By encouraging obedience, this system discourages creativity.

Old-fashioned ideas about music pedagogy are symptomatic of a larger societal pattern. Both *rank* and *privilege* are bestowed on those who are older, better educated, professionally successful. A mere child or someone in a lower socioeconomic position is often forced to humble herself, hold herself back, keep her good ideas hidden, and follow those who have more *assigned* power. Rob is making a change, but perhaps society itself must change. Perhaps the emblem of this transformation is the image of an eleven-year-old girl who knows what she needs and how she wants things to be, who is beginning to find the courage to speak up and teach others how she needs to be treated and how she needs to learn. It is our responsibility as teachers, as adults, and as members of society, to listen and heed the change.

It is radical to think that the teacher, rather than the student, should change. But a similar idea has been around for a long time in family therapy. The "identified patient" is the member of a family whom the family sees as the problem, as the one who needs to change. This person is viewed by the family therapist, though, as just one member of a troubled family. When the focus is taken away from the identified patient and the whole family makes a change, the identified patient is relieved and, often, her symptoms disappear.

In a music lesson, the student is identified as the one who must learn, who must change, who must adapt. If a student gives the teacher problems, then she is scolded, disliked, or ignored. Ruth had been causing her teacher problems for a long time. She was always like this, he complained. All of his attempts to change her did not work. Yet as soon as Rob stepped out of his role, she stopped resisting. Changing the system rendered her "symptom" unnecessary. Her message was starting to be heard.

Deep Democracy in Teaching

If we are deeply democratic, then we value and listen to *all* parts. In the teaching situation, the student has less power. The teacher normally decides what to teach, how to teach it, and how to evaluate whether it has been learned. Being deeply democratic would mean giving the student a say in this process, letting her in on the decisions that affect her education. Teachers may fear this change, but they would also benefit from it in the long run. For if the needs and ideas of students were taken into consideration, then much of the rebellion that is a normal part of education would be seen as creativity and used to further the teaching process.

I believe teachers would find that their educational goals, as well as the students', would be met if they worked together as a team. Deep democracy does not mean that the students take full control. This would be revolution with one side still being powerless. Rather, the idea is to support and value both sides, both sets of needs, both ideas about how, what, and when things should be done.

Following Two Courses at Once

Just as the student cannot simply replace the teacher in a music lesson, process work cannot replace time-tested teaching methods. Ignoring the wisdom and techniques passed down through generations of teaching would be, first of all, not democratic and, second, foolish. Process work is less a method of teaching music than it is a meta-model for dealing with the music lesson. By this I mean that process work provides a structure that helps us to understand and work with the complex interactions between student, teacher, and music. What we need is a synthesis of process work and existing teaching methods. One such synthesis occurred during Ruth's next piano lesson, a week after the experience described above.

It was early December and the annual Christmas concert was drawing closer. Ruth had tried to call Rob at home to ask him something about the preparations. He had not been home, so she left a message on his answering machine. When she walked into the lesson, she complained that he had not been at home when she wanted to talk to him. He said that he could never be sure when he would be at home. She said that he should have his time allotted, stick to his schedule, and know precisely when he would be home.

We can admire Ruth's strength and, simultaneously, sympathize with Rob. Looking from another perspective, we see two figures doing battle. One demanded that the other keep to a precise time schedule. The other rebelled, wanting to keep to its own rhythm and be free. At this point, the student was identified with the timekeeper and the teacher with the rebel.

Then she played the piano. He told her to play the piece in a slower tempo, but she refused, saying that she wanted to play it how she liked and not keep to his time. But, he said, when she played it so quickly she made too many mistakes, and this was not acceptable for the concert. The initial roles had already switched and now Ruth was resisting *Rob's* time demand. This was truly a field in which the roles were floating and not attached to a particular person.

The background fight was interfering with the lesson. Rob insisted that Ruth play in his tempo, and she pouted and did not play at all. This was certainly not helping either to prepare for the Christmas concert! His goal was that she be able to play the piece without mistakes, and he thought that the only way for her to do this would be to play it more slowly. Her goal was to be able to play the piece quickly. She thought it was boring when slow, and she liked the music for its excitement. They were at loggerheads due to their differing goals and the polarized roles that they unconsciously enacted.

It would have been possible to work with Ruth's mistakes. To do so would have helped her with her personal process, and may even have helped her to play quickly and without mistakes. But such an intervention would have ignored the background pattern that structured their interaction. Working with them as a system was the more powerful direction to take.

I mentioned that although they thought they were having a music lesson, they were actually in the middle of a fight between someone wanting to be exact and punctual and the other wanting to be free and wild. Rob saw that he, too, liked to be free to do things how and when he pleased. And Ruth agreed that she liked things to be precise, ordered, and on time. With the realization that they each experienced both sides of this polarization, the opposition de-escalated. Rob backed down and supported her to play the piece quickly. Ruth played in her own tempo, but then was disturbed that she still made mistakes, saying that it was not precise enough. She asked him to teach her to play both quickly and without errors. He proceeded to show her some techniques that would help her to reach her goal.

This outcome involved a true integration. Both figures were satisfied, because the free one learned to keep its own time and still be precise. By valuing their differing educational and musical goals (playing without mistakes vs. keeping the music fast and exciting), both were attained. The incomplete process from the last lesson (that she would teach him how to teach) completed itself. She was able to tell him exactly what she needed, and he was fluid enough—and talented enough—to teach her the thing she wanted to learn in a way that she could accept.

The ancient Taoist, Chuang Tsu, would call this "following two courses at once." Sometimes opinions and needs only seem to conflict because we are not in touch with the nature that underlies them. Chuang Tsu says that we "wear out [our] spirit and intelligence in order to unify things without knowing that they are already in agreement." Finding the Tao here meant discovering the background process: that teacher and student were already united by the fact that they shared the roles that seemed to separate them. Once they realized this, it was easy to find a solution to the conflict that was no longer a conflict.

Try This:

1. Remember your favorite teacher (music, art, creative writing, or whoever your favorite was).

2. What did you love about this teacher? A quality of being with you? Her precision? Her acceptance? Her challenging you? Write this down.

3. Remember the way she stood or sat during your lessons. Watch her carefully in your mind's eye, and hear her in your mind's ear. Study everything about her, including her movements, her tone of voice, the words she used.

4. Now become her. Stand or sit like her. Move like her. Use the same voice and words.

5. From the position of the teacher, look at your normal self. Look at your normal problems with music, creativity, expression, and life in general. What advice would you (the favorite teacher) have for your normal self? Write that down.

6. Go back to your normal self. What reaction do you have to this advice? If you like the advice, take it and act on it immediately. If not, say what you don't like about it.

7. Go back to the teacher role. What do you (the favorite teacher) have to say to your normal self's reaction?

8. Let these two roles ("you" and "the teacher") interact until both are happy.

9. Close your eyes and thank your teacher for visiting. Know that she can come whenever you need her.

Chapter 10

"That Horrible Sound!"
Freeing the Hated Voice

This chapter focuses on people who hate their own voices. You may not know that such people exist, or you may think that they have nothing to do with you. But have you ever been judgmental of the way you express yourself, or don't express yourself? Has anyone ever criticized you because they thought you should have expressed yourself differently than you did? Have you ever wished you could be more fluent, or eloquent, or powerful, or calm, or beautiful, or normal, or just fit in? If so, you have a lot in common with the people you are about meet. Their particular issues may seem on the surface to be unconnected to yours. Deep down, though, their struggle is about expression, about freedom, and about discovering and standing up for who they are.

Some people can't stand the sound of their own voices. They refuse to own an answering machine because they would have to record an outgoing message and hear themselves on tape. They tend to speak softly so as not to impose their supposedly unappealing voice on others, or even hear it themselves. Or they barely open their mouths, creating tense jaws and mumbled words, which only magnify the problem. Others are horrified that their own voice is so quiet, and try to make it stronger or louder. Still others can't stand their own accent, pitch, tone, or the way they laugh. You might be surprised how many people around you feel this way. You'll probably never hear about it, though, since they're often too ashamed to speak about it. In fact, this shame makes some people freeze up and stop expressing themselves altogether.

Voice teachers and speech therapists can help a lot by teaching people to use their voices "correctly." Many people get relief and live happier lives as a result. Some are not helped, though, and others feel subtly put down, because focusing on fixing their symptom only reinforces the belief that there is something wrong with them. The "cure," then, has the paradoxical effect of increasing their self-hatred, which may have been part of the problem in the first place.

Some of these people end up in my private practice or unintentional music seminars. They are hoping that a different approach to sound might somehow free them from their painful dilemma. My perspective is that any sound we make is music, and any disturbing sound we make is unintentional music. Whether it happens when we sing or speak or snore or cough is not important. The same attitudes and tools that help us to find meaning and value in our unwanted music can also help us to discover the mystery behind whatever sounds we make and hate.

Does that mean we have to amplify those horrible sounds? Don't we want to get rid of them? Well, if we can make ourselves sound the way we want to sound, great! But if we keep trying but can't seem to break the hold of those things we detest, why not embrace them?

Chuang Tsu shows the way with a story. Confucius (the foil and fool of many Taoist tales) was sitting beside a raging river when he saw an aged man apparently fall in. He told his disciples to run quickly and save the man, who would surely be drowned in the river's many whirlpools. By the time the disciples found him, though, the old man was drying himself on the shore. They brought him to Confucius, who was shocked that he had survived. The old man said that if he had fought against the whirlpool, it would have drowned him. Instead, when he felt himself being pulled down, he followed the whirlpool all the way to the bottom. At the bottom, it spit him back out. In the same way, fighting against our disturbing sounds may only increase their pull. As we will see, going into them—and listening to their message—is often the surest way out.

Buzz Off!

Having been a professional dancer and singer for seventeen years, Lucia was not inhibited about expressing herself on stage. But she had hated her speaking voice since the age of ten. Lucia's teacher used to tease her in front of the class and in the corridors of the school, saying that her voice sounded like the buzzing of a *besouro*, a kind of flying beetle. (She grew up in Brazil, where such beetles are common.) After this public humiliation, she had been ashamed of this buzzing quality whenever she spoke. She was even embarrassed to be talking about it in the seminar, although she knew many of the participants. This woman, whom I knew as being open and gregarious, seemed to fold into herself and shrink in front of my eyes.

At the start of our work, I asked Lucia to amplify the buzzing quality, and she did, but soon stopped, saying it was overwhelming. It "took her over" and was unpleasant. But still she decided to explore it further. Her whole head started to buzz, putting her into an altered state. As she went on, her head felt bigger and her entire body started growing, she said. Her eyes glazed over as she went deeper into a trance; the buzzing increased and her arms started moving as she grew and grew. Now, arms raised above her head, she went up onto her toes. She was flying, she said. She felt huge.

Up on her toes, arms in the air and buzzing loudly, Lucia looked me straight in the eye and said, "I *am* the besouro."

I assumed the role of her old teacher and said that her voice sounded stupid. She took her raised hands and pinched me hard on my chest with her "pincers." This sudden and strong movement scared me and I pulled back, speechless. It was impossible to stay in the critical role in the face of such an awesome creature. Lucia said that her pincers had deflated the teacher. She was no longer in a trance and felt empowered by the experience.

The next day Lucia reported that, for the first time since childhood, she liked her speaking voice. When I contacted her years later, she told me that our work had made a long-lasting change in her feeling about her voice. Ever since then she has been able to listen to recordings of public speeches she makes. Before that, she was given cassettes of her talks but never dared to play them.

By encouraging Lucia to buzz on purpose, I was hoping to put her in touch with who or what was making that sound. Like Elaine's slapstick mummies in chapter 4, the besouro was an ally for Lucia, an awesome power that followed her around her entire life, buzzing in her voice. During the session, she experienced it as taking her over. This process was similar to a spirit possession, in which a shaman goes into a trance and allows the spirit to enter her. Lucia resisted this at first. But when she went deeper into the buzz-induced trance and opened herself to the besouro, embraced it, singing its song and dancing its dance, the ally gave her power far beyond her mortal abilities. The hated buzzing transformed her into an invincible opponent.

Clouds of War

Maria loathed her voice. Unlike Lucia, she had no objective reason, no childhood critic who had turned her against herself. To

Maria, though, the reason was clear. Her voice was simply disgusting. (I had known her for years and had never thought twice about her voice, so it was obviously a subjective experience.) She could not bear to hear herself on tape. When I recorded a few minutes of our session and played it for her, she covered her ears and started making loud noises so she would not have to listen. We both thought this was funny, but when I played the tape again she screamed and stuck her fingers in her ears. She begged me not to play it anymore, saying that she had already discovered what was so disturbing. She could not stand the *tone* of her voice because it sounded to her like something that was hiding. I asked her to make her voice sound even more like that. As she did, her throat constricted and nothing came out of her mouth. She was unable to make the sound anymore due to this symptom.

Maria had come to an edge. Although many body symptoms are expressions of secondary processes, this one came at exactly the moment she was trying to intentionally do the thing that disturbed her. She was just crossing the border of her identity when something inside of her reacted strongly, creating the tightness in her throat and preventing any further exploration of her hated vocal timbre. There was no way to go forward in the "normal" ways described in this book. The only way was to explore the symptom itself and to discover its relationship to her voice.

She paid close attention to the feeling in her throat, so that she could reproduce that precise experience with her hands. Maria then tightly squeezed a pillow in the same way that her throat felt squeezed. The pillow got smaller and smaller. She said she wanted to make it two dimensional, but did not know why. I asked her to make up a fairy tale about "the one who is squeezing." She said that an evil spirit entered a room and squeezed out the life from a little girl. The girl was suffocated. There was no room for her. Why did the spirit do this? Maria answered that the spirit was like an invisible cloud that searched for littleness or joy, and then killed it. Why, I asked? What was the cloud's story? She said it was the cloud of war, the spirit of war. This cloud did not leave space for anything joyful or little or anything that was not like war.

It came out that Maria's family had suffered a lot during the Second World War in Poland. Although Maria had been born after the war, a heavy atmosphere still hung over her family. Her grandfather would tell stories and everyone would sit around listening solemnly. No space was given for happiness or singing. It was not that her family would have been upset or scolded someone for singing. It just never happened because the atmosphere of war and suffering did not leave room for anything else.

Maria had never thought about this before our session. She was shocked that something that had happened long before her birth could have had such a strong influence on her life. She realized that by hating her own voice, she was unconsciously identifying with the spirit of war. Like the cloud, she did not give space to the joy that had been crushed in her when she was a child. Although she saw the importance of grieving and suffering, she did not want to continue killing the little girl inside her.

When we played the tape again, she was able to listen, and she even liked her voice a little bit. She said she felt compassion for it. Then she suddenly covered her ears. I said, "Hello, Cloud of War! You hate that little girl!" She took her hands away from her ears and was able to listen again. It was just a matter of awareness. Once she realized that just the cloud, not her whole self, hated her voice, she could make a conscious choice in every moment whether she wanted to support the cloud or the girl. Maria happily announced the next week that she had noticed again and again how the cloud suffocated her joy, and that each time she had noticed it, the joy began to live.

War had been like an unseen member of Maria's family. She had inhaled it with each breath, swallowed it with each bite, taken it for granted without even knowing it was there. It told her in silent whispers that having fun was forbidden. Her voice was like a leak in an otherwise tightly closed container. A joyous little girl leaked out of the restrictive borders of her family's dominant mood, like a squeak of air coming out of a balloon. The cloud had no room for this child and wanted her dead. But the human spirit is strong. Although under constant threat, the little one lived an autonomous existence, making her home in the tone of Maria's voice. For many years Maria had rejected the girl, not realizing that she herself had become the cloud of war. Now, by learning to love her own voice, she was taking her life back into her own joyous hands.

The Roar of a Lioness

The spirit of war had limited Maria's expressiveness and spontaneity without her even realizing it was an issue for her. Sometimes, though, we are fully aware of the thing that puts us down but we feel helpless in the face of it. Having experienced the intransigent nature of oppression, we stop thinking that we can change the world. This leads us to a state of hopelessness, which acts like a damp rag over our feelings and reactions. We stop even trying and focus instead on the day-to-day business of our lives. But the dreaming process never sleeps. Even if we do not react, our bodies do. Sometimes our vocal symptoms are trying to show us new ways of dealing with old and painful problems.

Sylvia came in complaining of a chronic cough. It had been pestering her for many months. She had been to doctors and taken many medicines, including several courses of antibiotics, all to no avail. Actually, what she called a cough was not your average cough. It was more that she often cleared her throat very loudly. I would even describe it less as clearing her throat and more as a loud and repeated throaty vocalization. I tried to ask her about what was happening in her throat that made her want to "cough." I thought that the coughing was a reaction to some experience she did not like, perhaps a tickling or a build-up of phlegm. She was not at all interested in that approach. Without paying much attention to my question, she said it was the coughing that she hated. "That horrible sound!" I followed her interest and asked her about that horrible sound.

Clearing her throat again and wincing, she said it was loud and ugly. It was so rough and raspy, she continued, not at all pretty. I asked her to intentionally make it even louder, rougher, and raspier. Being a sweet and gentle woman who usually spoke quietly, she was very shy and only made tentative attempts. I encouraged her by making loud and raspy noises myself. This made it easier for her. Together we made progressively louder and rougher noises. She said it sounded like lions roaring. We roared at each other, and her hands came up like claws. We played like this for a while, both of us having lots of fun. I asked what the lioness was roaring about. Sylvia said the lioness was fighting for her place, protecting what was hers. She said the lioness would not give up what was hers and would fight to the death for it. What would Sylvia fight for, I wondered aloud. What is being taken away from her?

At this moment the game stopped. Sylvia got very serious and said the whole society tries to take from her the right to love her girlfriend. They think they know what is right, what is good for her. They put her down in subtle and overt ways. Her family refuses to acknowledge her relationship. The Church says she is immoral. People try to fix her up with interesting men. The litany of hurts was long and infuriating. But Sylvia just stood there, shrugged her shoulders, and asked rhetorically, "What can you do?"

Homophobia had oppressed her for so long that she could no longer even imagine reacting. Here was a dynamic woman, active and successful in many areas of her life, reduced to depression, hopelessness, and inertia. I repeated the question, "What *can* you do?" hoping to evoke some glimmer of an answer inside of her. There was nothing. Her usually sparkling eyes were dull. The weight of culture, religion, time, and convention had stopped Sylvia in her tracks. But it could not stop her dreaming process. Sylvia coughed loudly.

Here was the answer to her question. "That horrible sound" knew what to do. I asked Sylvia how the lioness would react to those people who put her down. She roared at me. Hearing this as positive feedback, I took the role of the homophobe. I told her that she was immoral, that I knew a great guy for her who would love to ..."AAAAAAAAAIIIIIIIIII!!!!!!!" Sylvia's scream stopped me dead. The room still rang with its echo. She stood there in shock. She had rarely ever raised her voice, much less let out a bloodcurdling scream like that. Something inside her was shifted by that scream. She had discovered her strength and her ability to let it out in a convincing way. She knew she had to fight like a lioness for what was rightfully hers. And she knew she *could* fight.

Rather than get rid of it, as Sylvia had already tried unsuccessfully to do, we treated her "cough" as unintentional music. Valuing and exaggerating its disturbing qualities let the lioness out of her cage and into the world. Which is exactly where she was needed.

A Triumphant Turn

These women all suffered from vocal disturbances. Another way of saying this is that these women were disturbed because their voices did not fit into their (or our) ideas about how someone should sound. Their voices were imprisoned by concepts of what is pleasant or acceptable. They were too soft, too loud, too different. But these aberrations from the norm were expressions of each woman's individuality, of some not quite stifled, essential aspect of her nature. Letting the strangeness "sing" liberated that hidden essence so it could be heard and seen in all its glory, whether it was huge and fierce, or tiny and joyous. Hated sounds became songs of freedom.

These women were trapped in other ways as well. Public humiliation, oppression, and war had left them ashamed, hopeless, and filled with self-hatred. All of this effectively strangled their natural reactions and expressiveness, their inborn joy, their spontaneity. They never guessed that the sounds they wanted to lock up were, in fact, keys to unlock their own prison cells. Freeing their voices paradoxically freed the women themselves.

Many of us have had, or continue to have, experiences that inhibit our expression, our creativity, our musicality. These experiences block our true nature from expressing itself and make us feel hopeless and worthless. But Nature is not defeated. It waits in our double signals for a moment of awareness. Then it rises like a phoenix from the flames. The trauma that dampens the spirit can be transformed into a triumph of the spirit.

In the park near the street where I lived for five years, on the edge of what used to be the Warsaw Ghetto, is one of my favorite trees. It stands at a forty-five degree angle to the ground. Many years ago it was probably blown down by the wind. Or maybe a bolt of lightning, in a fit of desire, licked his fiery lips and said, *"You're gonna be mine."* However it happened, the tree is now mostly hollow and leaning heavily toward the earth. Big gaping holes show its blackened, empty core.

When I first caught sight of it, I felt a pang of sorrow, being sure it was practically dead. Then I noticed a twist about two-thirds of the way up the trunk, where it makes a victorious turn and reaches for the sky. Somehow the sap went through and around those wounds and rose beyond adversity. The tree wears its scars proudly, a testimony to how far it has come.

It doesn't try to fill holes that can never be filled, where small animals now make their home. No, it directs its energy toward growth. And that tree's contrasts—bent and straight, scarred and triumphant, holed and whole—make it that much more beautiful, courageous, authentic, moving, extraordinary. Now the tree dances with its fate as the life within flows ever higher.

If we follow the individual wisdom and uniqueness in each of us, we will find expression and creativity beyond our wildest dreams. And perhaps the most creative project of all is opening ourselves to what we are closed to, going deeply into whatever pulls us off our intended course, trusting in and unfolding the beauty that is trying to emerge.

Try This:

1. Remember a time when you were told to shut up, that you should not express yourself, that you should not be creative, that you could not be creative, that you are not creative (artistic, musical, intelligent, etc.), or a time when you were scolded for being creative, expressive, or just for being yourself.

2. Tell that story. (If you are alone, write it down.)

3. Tell (or write) what you did back then, how you reacted.

4. Now you have a choice about how you want to continue. Either
   A) Take over the energy, sound, movement of the shutter-upper. What did he/she sound like? Do this now, but without content. Just get into that energy, without using the specific words that hurt you. When you are deeply into this energy, ask yourself whether there is something about this energy that you could use in your life? Could it help you in your expression? Could you use it to be creative? Could you use it in an interaction with the critical figure?
   B) What were you told not to do? What sound, movement, etc. in particular? Do this more now. Exaggerate it and let it express however it wants to express. Welcome this forbidden expressiveness back into your life. Say yes to it! Enjoy it!

If you can think of absolutely no negative experiences, and you were really supported as a child and adult, you are lucky indeed! In that case, remember a time when you were very supported. Tell (or write) that story. Act like the person who supported you. Play this out and really feel the energy of the supporter. Learn to support yourself now, in your expression, in your creativity, and in your whole life.

Part V

Living Creativity

*The moment when we are both asleep and awake
… is the one moment of creation.*

–William Butler Yeats

Chapter 11
Unintentional Art

I was lucky to learn at an early age about the positive effects of the unintentional on art, watching my mother carve sculptures out of wood. She would start with an idea of the form she wanted to create. Sometimes, though, a large knot in the wood would hamper her plans, forcing her to rework the piece. This inevitably made the sculpture even more beautiful, as the impenetrable knot became a shoulder pushing forward or some other previously unintended focal point of the piece. Like the diamond cutter (mentioned in the Introduction) who engraved a rose around a deep scratch, she took the problem and turned it into art.

Anything can be transformed into art. Masterpieces have been created out of fine marble dug from quarries and ordinary objects found in junkyards. The deepest love and the most terrifying nightmare are equal in the eyes of the muse. In my opinion, the essential ingredient of creativity is not the medium, nor the subject, nor the artist's tools, nor her skill. I think it is something far more mysterious than that. My purpose here is not to define that ineffable quality, but rather to help you to come into contact with it.

Michelangelo said that his sculptures were already in the stone, waiting to be released by his chisel. How can we find what is already in front of us, or inside of us? How can we get in touch with that unexpressed something that is trying to come through us and into the world?

In my experience, the unintentional holds the key. We have already seen that unintentional music helps us to play and sing in ways we never could have imagined. It frees us from our boxes, opens our ears to what we don't mean to be playing, and helps us to find the music that wants to be played. It brings us into contact with a deeper expression that is original and authentic.

This can happen in any creative medium when you follow the unintentional. The same concepts, the same tools, and the same attitudes discussed throughout this book can be directly translated to any artistic or creative project. Be with what is. Notice what you are trying to do, and also what is happening outside of your intention. Notice the "mistake," or whatever is different from the rest, and exaggerate it. It's really so simple.

The challenging part is to love whatever happens, to stay with it, and to trust that it will lead you where you ultimately want to go. The unintentional can lead you to a new creativity and a new expression. It can bring you into contact with the feelings behind the technique, the realness behind the mask. It can help you to explore the unknown, and to bring whatever you find there back into your art, or back into whatever you decide to create.

Creativity isn't restricted to making art or music. You can be creative in your thinking. You can solve problems in creative ways. Gardening or cooking or storytelling or telling jokes or doing math or cutting hair or even walking can be creative projects. In the following examples, the unintentional is unfolded in recognizably "artistic" forms. Feel free, though, to follow "what happens" everywhere in your life. Everything you do can be creative. The unintentional will be happy to lend a hand.

Visual Art: Squiggle to Freedom

Bernie wanted help with his drawing. He had graduated from an art academy, but was still not happy with his art. Sitting by the water, Bernie showed me the sketch he was working on of a bridge in the distance. It was an exact representation of the bridge and the water below. Every line was perfectly placed. The curves were gentle and the straight lines could have been drawn with a ruler. Except one. In one corner of the drawing was a short squiggle. It leaked slightly out of the carefully executed outline of the bridge. It did not fit with the rest of the picture, yet was so small it was very hard to notice.

One of my teachers, Max Schupbach, used to say that process work is like fishing. When you notice a signal, that is the fish nibbling on the bait. The rest of the work is just getting the fish into the boat. This squiggle was the nibble.

I encouraged Bernie to make a new sketch of the bridge, using only squiggly lines. Not straight or gracefully curved, but short, erratically curved lines that did not fit into the structured outline of his original picture. The result was striking. His drawing became impressionistic, revealing a bridge as if seen through the water, as if it were itself a reflection of the bridge in water. The bridge was certainly there, but so was a feeling, a mood that had been missing in the first realistic rendering. Bernie was moved. He said that the teachers at the academy had taught him very well how to be a perfect draftsperson, an exact recorder of his surroundings. But they had not taught him to put something of himself in his drawings.

Let's study this for a moment, to see how the tools we use to work with unintentional music can be translated to another medium. The squiggle was a double signal, something different than the rest of what Bernie was drawing. What made it different? *Size:* It was much shorter than any other line on the paper. *Line:* The irregular twists were a sharp contrast to the gradual curves or straight lines. *Form:* Disturbing the overall form, the squiggle broke out of the carefully copied outline. Size, line, and form could be considered subchannels of the visual channel (see chapter 7). We could also include color, light/darkness, depth, and texture. While working with sculpture we would have to take other qualities into account as well, such as consistency, hardness, and weight. You may have other ideas of how to differentiate the visual (or any) channel. The important thing is not which categories you use or whether they are objectively correct; rather, it is whether they help you to structure your awareness and to describe what you see in a way that is useful, nonjudgmental, and noninterpretive.

Once we notice the details of a signal, it is easy to unfold it. The interventions in chapter 8 could be transferred to a new channel, or at least as many methods could be discovered for visual art or any other medium. Bernie globalized the "mistake," making it happen all over the page. The result was an evocative picture unlike any he had learned to draw. His squiggle had become his teacher.

Dance: The Fall from Grace

Linda, a professional dancer, did an improvisation in front of the group in a movement seminar. Her motions were graceful and refined, her face smiling. Somehow, though, her dance did not touch me. It struck me as pretty on the outside yet not connected with the dancer herself. Since this was a subjective opinion, I kept it to myself.

Watching for double signals, I noticed a few moments when she seemed to almost lose her balance but then, using her considerable skills, recovered by adding another graceful turn or leap. I was not even sure of my perception, so flowing were her movements. Linda admitted there had been a couple of moments of imbalance. She said that she had suffered from this problem throughout her dancing career, but had learned techniques and tricks to mask it in front of the audience. Linda agreed to follow the imbalance, to allow it to express itself. Her dance of polished arcs and turns became a bit stiff and jerky. She even had a couple of near falls. But she still did not allow herself to do it wholly. She said that she did not want it to be ugly, that she had spent her life trying to be beautiful and make beautiful movements.

This was an edge, the limit of her identity as a dancer and a person. Given society's focus on beauty, it is understandable that Linda would not want to be ugly. But perhaps "ugly" was just the primary process' description of a still unknown secondary process. Taking a deep breath, Linda decided to momentarily abandon her ideal and step into the mystery.

Dancing again, her movements became very jerky. She even fell down once, then gracefully spun on the floor and leaped up. She realized that this leap was a return to her normal way of dancing, and tried again to follow the lack of balance and jerkiness. She fell again, this time without a graceful recovery. Continuing on the floor, she realized that the jerkiness was, in fact, a slight pause between movements.

Amplifying that pause, she stopped altogether, sitting slumped on the floor and looking down. I gently encouraged her to stay with her motionlessness and notice what was happening inside of her. She said she could not notice anything and was afraid that nothing was inside her. I suggested that she could believe in the "nothing" that was there. Maybe something would grow out of it. Or maybe nothing would come of it, but that emptiness was what was real in the moment.

After a long time she softly said that she felt sad but that she should not feel this feeling. It was not pretty. It did not go along with the beautiful and happy movements that she was supposed to make as a dancer. I asked Linda to allow the nothingness or her feelings to direct her movements. Normally *she* makes the movements, but now she could be *moved by* whatever was inside of her. She said she was afraid that she would never move. In that case, I suggested, just be still; but if there is a movement inside, let it move you. For a long time Linda was still. Then, finally, she did move.

This was very different from her first improvisation. Her motions were slow and filled with feeling, though not necessarily pretty. It was not a mere performance. It was an expression of her *self.* It seemed that every movement was filled from the inside, was a living necessity. Gone was the beautiful but frozen smile that had accompanied her first dance. In its place was a natural and transparent face that showed every change of emotion as she let her insides lead the way. Everyone in the room could feel the emotional depth and authenticity of her dance.

Here, too, a double signal showed the way. Here, too, an edge (this time, reinforced by cultural norms about beauty) blocked the path to wholeness. Sidestepping ideas about what dance should look like, Linda unfolded her lack of balance into jerkiness, then nothingness, and eventually into deep feeling and true expression. Was this self-discovery or art? Here, too, the answer is yes.

Poetry: Touching the Mystery

Anita came into the middle of the circle crying. It was a creativity seminar, she said, but she was not creative at all. She was "good for nothing." The only things she knew how to do were cook and clean the house. She had spent years working on her master's thesis but could not finish it because of her conviction that she could never create anything. Tears ran down her face as seminar participants scrambled to find enough tissues. "Maybe you are good for nothing," I said, after giving her a chance to blow her nose, "but is there anything you *like* to do?" Anita said she liked to read, and that her favorite author was Umberto Eco. I asked what was special about his writing. She closed her eyes and said with a far-off voice that he writes about the mystery. Then she cried again and said that she could never know anything about the mystery and she could never create anything.

There was something about the way she closed her eyes and said the word *mystery* that was intriguing. I asked a woman sitting nearby to write down, word for word, whatever Anita said from then on. When I inquired further about the mystery, Anita closed her eyes again. Her descriptions came out little by little. "It is a ball," she said, "high up." When she stopped talking, I also paused, but then gently asked her to say more. "It is ... beautiful." Whenever she got to an edge, I softly repeated her last statement and asked what she meant by it. What slowly emerged was a song of yearning, of longing for the mystery that she could not touch.

It is a ball ... high up
it is ... beautiful
shimmering
perfect ...

unattainable

One can try to approach it
but it slips away

It is fascinating
sparkling
spinning ...
It simply ... is

I'll never get there
I cannot
I don't have enough courage
enough power
enough strength

I'd like to embrace it
be within it
live within it ... I'd be happy

There—is beautiful, colorful
there—is movement
there—are different planes
they turn and penetrate one another
there—are colors, smells
all of that—is alive
bewitching

There—are only the chosen ones

A great sorrow stirs within me
but at the same time, joy that I can speak about it
it is important that I can tell about it

I'd like to let myself . . .
permit myself . . . to reach it
or maybe believe that I deserve it
that I can
that I deserve

People—if they really desire
if they really want something, really desire it
have courage

if they let themselves
if they give themselves permission

After a time, she opened her eyes. The person who had written down her words read them slowly. Anita did not understand. What was this woman reading? It took a few moments for her to realize that these were, in fact, her own words. Listening once again, she could not believe it. She had written a poem about the mystery. She had done exactly the thing she was sure she could never do.

Months later, when her poem was published in a journal along with an article about the seminar, Anita cried with joy. She also proudly gave me a copy of her completed master's thesis, for which she had received the highest mark.

Anita believed she was nothing compared to those others who could create, nothing in the face of the unattainable mystery. Yet in her suffering was the very experience she sought. Her longing itself was the seed of her creativity. When this was held with loving attention, it unfolded like a flower that slowly starts to bloom. As Rilke would say, the summer did indeed come. Life did not let her fall.

Writing: Right on Target

I had a client who spent months passionately working on a writing project. We often spoke during our sessions about the problems he was having expressing what he wanted to say. Once John brought an essay-in-progress to our session and read it aloud. Employing mostly long, compound sentences, he used logic and reasoning to get his points across. But he was not satisfied. Something was missing. The pages were filled with long paragraphs of uninterrupted flow. At the bottom of the last page, though, was something different. There were a few bullets. They looked like this:

· Here was one idea.

· Here was another.

· And yet another.

Each of these bulleted points contained a concise statement of an issue that John had not yet addressed. They were notes to himself to help him remember what to write next. They looked very different from the long sentences and paragraphs of the essay itself. The word *bullet* (which he used) denotes something fast, explosive. I encouraged him to write the essay in bullet-like style. When he did, a remarkable change happened. His sentences shortened. He stopped building logical arguments. He expressed one point clearly. Then went on to the next point. His passion shined through the words. His writing became crisp. Clear. Powerful. Explosive.

Theater: Celestial Navigation

A group of us entered a Chinese restaurant in Virginia after the first day of a weekend seminar on creativity. I asked Cynthia to sit next to me. An award-winning playwright and actor as well as a powerful singer, she had impressed me three years earlier at a seminar on unintentional music. Now she wanted help with her newest play, and I knew she had not yet received the focus she needed. I was excited at the prospect of being a part of her creative process. We huddled together with another participant, Kevyn, at one corner of the table and got to work.

Cynthia's as yet unwritten play was to be called "Celestial Navigation." The main character, Claire, is a forty-something businesswoman who gives up everything to follow her passion for sailing. She learns about celestial navigation, how to chart a course by using the stars. Cynthia explained to me that you have to find a fixed point in the sky—any fixed object; it does not matter which. Then you can find where you are in relationship to this heavenly object. I asked about the symbolism of celestial navigation. Since it was such a major theme, what did it mean? She did not know yet, but had another problem that was more pressing.

The question remained with me, though. There had to be some significance, some reason for this key image. My college days studying theater and literature came back to me like a familiar scent on a warm breeze. I used to love the search for interwoven threads of hidden meaning. But this was no classic already analyzed by legions of academics. The playwright had not touched pen to paper. She herself did not yet know the reason for her fascination with celestial navigation. My curiosity was piqued. Sadly for me, however, Cynthia's attention was elsewhere. Like a hunting dog reined in from the chase, a part of my mind stayed with the riddle as we focused on the spot where she felt stuck.

The play's main focus was to be Claire; her male counterpart was still unclear. "I have many ideas and no good ideas," she said. "The man feels flat." The three of us started to brainstorm. Cynthia was thinking of including William Shakespeare in her cast of characters. She felt that his poetry, and maybe that of other poets, should be included in the play. Her voice dropped and her eyes seemed to focus on something far in the distance as she spoke of poetry. The ancient Polynesians, she told us, learned celestial navigation from poetry passed down through the generations. Poetry would have to be central. I pressed her to say why this was so important to her.

"Poets," she said with tears in her eyes, "can move events and people with their words." I said that Shakespeare and other poets were secondary for Cynthia. She projected her own poetic abilities onto them. She could write poetry for the play, I suggested, in addition to whatever Shakespeare she wanted to include. The whole play could be written as poetry, or parts of it. She herself could move people and events with her words. Cynthia's eyes opened wide.

Tears flowed again when she talked about following one's dreams. "Sometimes people do not follow their dreams," she lamented, "because they are following other people's dreams." This was a challenge for Claire, who gives up her career in order to sail, in spite of the advice and concern of her family. Why, I wondered aloud, did that touch Cynthia so?

By this time, everyone had finished eating. The waiters were looking awkwardly in our direction, uncomfortable with Cynthia's emotions. Companions spoke about going home, but I wanted to keep talking about the play. I felt we were onto something interesting, and I still did not understand the deeper meaning of celestial navigation. Cynthia, Kevyn, and I decided to go to a friendlier restaurant for the next round of creative discussion. As the group split up, the seminar organizer informed me that Cynthia had decided to leave the next morning. I was surprised that she was not staying the entire weekend. Had I fooled myself by thinking that she had appreciated my work?

As the three of us settled into our new restaurant and ordered drinks, I asked Cynthia why she was leaving. The story she told took me by complete surprise. Three years earlier, she explained, she had been so moved by the unintentional music seminar (and especially, as fate would have it, by the session I had done there with Kevyn), that she had considered becoming my apprentice. I had, just at that time, decided to move to Poland to teach process work. Cynthia had been very impressed that I was following my calling, and she had thought of following me to Warsaw to study with me.

I listened with amazement as she said that she had thought about it for three years and had now come to the seminar to "bring Lane into the present." Rather than still living with this old image of me and my work, she wanted to discover who I really was. Now that she had seen me, she realized that I do what I do, and she does what she does. She should not follow me but instead must be herself. She was thrilled we were talking about the play together, but felt no need to stay for the rest of the workshop. After three years, it was time to leave.

After getting over my shock, I realized that this explanation was very connected to her play. I had been wondering why Cynthia was so moved when talking about the importance of Claire following her heart. I now understood that Cynthia had been on the verge of following my dream rather than her own. I guessed that this danger had arisen at other times in her life as well. We spoke of how a woman often follows a man, adapting her life to his work and dreams. I suggested that the male character (the captain or boat builder she had told me about) could be someone who Claire wants to follow, but that she could decide to follow her own dreams instead.

Suddenly I understood the deeper meaning of celestial navigation. She (Claire/Cynthia) chooses a fixed object in the sky (Captain/Lane). But this is not the thing that she needs to follow. It is just an arbitrarily chosen, fixed point that shows her where *she* is on the Earth. The important thing is not to follow the planet or the Captain or Lane, but rather to find herself through them. Following me to Poland would have been following my calling, not her own. She needed to be the captain of her own destiny. This resonated deeply with Cynthia. It also helped her to understand her own experience over the past three years and gave her ideas about what to do with Claire and the male characters as well. Art and reality were co-creating each other. Early the next morning, Cynthia drove home to follow her own heart and write her play.

A month later, back in Warsaw, I got a package in the mail. It was the first draft of "Celestial Navigation." Although most of the dialogue is prose, a lot of it is poetic. Some is pure poetry. In fact, "Poetry" is a character (played by Cynthia). In this passage, she describes celestial navigation.

Forget
Forget   *How the earth spins around the sun*
Forget   *How the stars*

hang
motionless
inconceivable distances   away
A distance only understood by
Mathematicians
And poets.

Instead

Remember
Remember   the earth is the center
Remember   you are the center
and all around you spins the sun, the moon, the planets
all the heavenly bodies

The heart knows that you are the center of this pre-Copernican
Universe
Even if the mind says   you   are   not

Remember . . . the center
Only then can you navigate the wild, dark sea

Shakespeare was no longer a projection but a part of her. Cynthia wrote to me, "Thinking I could dare to write poetry was a gift."

She also incorporated much of our discussion into the play. Simply put, the main plot centers around Claire (also played by Cynthia), who has decided she wants to sail. She meets Captain Emory, who teaches her the basics and pronounces her seaworthy. He also encourages her to trust the stars over technology and thus she begins an outer and inner discovery of the magic of celestial navigation. Claire meets a boat builder named Patrick, who needs a crew. She signs on and gets what she thinks is everything she wants. But Patrick changes his plans. Rather than navigating the seas, he prepares to sail through inland waterways. When Claire receives an invitation to cross the ocean on another boat, she is faced with a difficult choice. Should she follow Patrick? Or should she follow her dream to cross the blue water? She is conflicted. Then, drawing on the wisdom of celestial navigation, she understands.

> *My eye*
> *Mistook you for my destination*
> *And now I see, that you were for*
> *A time my star on which I took my sights.*

Claire decides to follow her own course, not his. She leaves Patrick, much like Cynthia left me after the first day of the seminar, free to chart her own destiny.

Try This:

1. Take a pencil and paper.

2. Close your eyes. Put your hand on the paper so you have a general feeling about where the outline of the paper is.

3. Think of something, anything, and draw it with your eyes closed.

4. Open your eyes and look at the paper. You will see something completely different from what you thought you had drawn.

5. Forget the original notion of what you thought you had drawn. See what you have really drawn. Imagine into that.

6. Now, with your eyes open, continue drawing. Dropping your original concept, embellish what is actually on the paper.

7. Is there anything different about this drawing from the way you normally draw? Is there a new quality?

8. Now take another piece of paper and intentionally use this new quality in your next drawing.

Chapter 12

Loving the Block: And Other Surprising Ways to Unlock Your Creative Potential

You might be thinking, "This all sounds fine if you are in the creative flow, if something unintentional is already emerging. But what if you are blocked? What if nothing comes out? How do you start?"

Start with what is. In my experience, the guru, the ultimate teacher, is whatever is actually happening. In the last chapter, Anita suffered because she thought she could never create and could never know the mystery. Suffering and longing were present, so I encouraged her to be *with* suffering and longing. From that unlikely beginning, she created a poem about the mystery and ultimately was able to complete her master's thesis. Wherever you are, be there. But be there with awareness. That is the way to support the creative process that is trying to happen.

What stops you, personally, from creating? Maybe you are jealous of your friends who are creative, and you spend all your time focusing on them instead of doing your own thing. Or you might criticize yourself mercilessly. Or you sit around procrastinating, or pacing the floor, when you "should" be working on a creative project. Process work says "yes" to all of that. Notice the unproductive direction you are heading—and go even further in that direction. I know it sounds crazy, but it works. Being blocked is boring, but when you learn to love the block, to become the thing blocking you, then life starts to get interesting. The fastest way out is to really go into it. The quickest way to tap into your creative potential is to start where you are right now.

You may say you don't have a creative potential. Baloney. Everyone does. I have never seen a single person, in all of my work around the globe, who was not able to be creative when given love, attention, and a few simple tools. The most basic tool is an appreciation of *whatever is happening*.

In this chapter you will find more ideas and tools that you can use whenever your creative process is blocked. Though far from exhaustive, the following material covers some of the main problems I have encountered in my own creative ebbs and flows and in those of the many people with whom I've worked. Make your own list. Notice what seems to lead you away from creativity, and follow that. As long as you're blocked, you always have someplace to start.

Jealousy

Being only human, we're not always so happy when those around us are creative. We might get jealous when someone clinches a book deal or records a CD, or even writes a song or paints a painting. Maybe it gets under our skin when a friend tells good stories, knows how to cut hair, cooks well, or has a beautiful garden. Most people think they shouldn't be jealous. It's an emotion that gets a bad rap in our culture. But there is nothing wrong with jealousy, as long as it is used well. That forbidden twinge is a compass, pointing you in the direction you could be heading. Instead of secretly wishing your friend (or enemy) would hit the mother of all dry spells, why not do whatever she's doing? Observe her, or even interview her. Find out how she does it.

Before starting to write this book, I was upset because my friend Arny had already written over ten of them. I couldn't stand that he took what seemed to me at the time like whole summers just to write. What a luxury, I thought, sharpening my claws. My dreams had been telling me to write, and Arny had often encouraged me, but I thought I could never take so much time away from my "real work." And anyway, I had no idea how to go about writing a book. So I stewed in my own juices. It didn't help our friendship either. Then I thought, wait a minute! I'm not upset that he does it. I'm upset that I *don't*.

So I called him up and asked him how to go about it. And, generous friend that he is, he told me in detail. I followed his advice to the letter, from the first draft, through the editing process, and even to the point of finding a publisher. Now, instead of jealousy, I feel incredible love and gratitude. It's good to remember, though, that this whole project started with a green monster growing in my belly.

Who sparks your jealousy? If you have the courage, call that person on the phone and tell her that you want to be like her. Ask her how she does it. Of course, you'd have to swallow your pride. But, if she is open hearted, or if your honesty throws her off guard, she may even tell you her secrets.

If you don't want to call that person, or can't do it for some reason, then study her in your mind's eye. If you've never met her, imagine what she's like. Watch her doing the thing you are jealous of. Sit or stand like she does. Move like her. Imagine how she feels when she is creating, and feel those feelings in your body. Now use that energy to work on your own creative project.

Inner Jealousy

You may also find yourself the victim of another kind of jealousy. Shamans and traditional healers know that sickness can sometimes be caused by a person or spirit being jealous of you and cursing you. This is not as far fetched as it sounds. I see it all the time in my work. Musicians, artists, and folks from all walks of life complain about being stuck, stagnated, unable to grow, unable to create. They complain of depression, fatigue, and illness. Sometimes no amount of process work seems to help. It may look like things are going well for a while. It may even seem like the person is just about to bloom—and then she collapses again in a heap on the chair and says she just can't do it.

Very often, it turns out that an inner figure is jealous of the person's growth. This inner figure seems malicious, but "it" may simply be upset that the person can do something that it can't, and so it blocks any further development or success. Teaching this inner figure how to play and create can break the "spell" and free the person's creativity. An example will make this perhaps strange notion easy to understand.

Sue was a painter who sold her work at galleries in the city where she lived. She came to me in a funk, her work at a standstill. She could not pick up a brush, and she sat around her house all day in a depression. No matter what we tried, nothing worked. The depression was stronger than both of us. Rather than fighting against it, I decided to let it take us down to the depths. I sat there with Sue, quiet and sad. I told her that nothing would work. She agreed. She said that life is just hard. It is filled with suffering. All you can do is survive. I saw a hint of understanding in Sue's eyes and asked her about it. She said that this sounded exactly like her deceased grandmother. Sue's grandmother, I learned, had suffered a lot. She had lived through horrendous times and, by the time Sue knew her, was an old and bitter woman. I asked Sue to act like her grandmother, while I interacted with her. The grandmother launched into her lament about how hard life is.

"Yes, that's true," I said respectfully to Grandmother, "but Sue does not want to only have a hard life."

"That Sue!" Grandmother screamed. "She wastes all her time with that stupid painting! She should forget that nonsense once and for all and get serious."

"Dear Grandmother, I see that you are upset with Sue. And I understand you. Your life was indeed difficult and painful. I bet you were never able to do something so frivolous as paint."

"I should say not," she harrumphed.

"Did you ever wish you could?" I asked tentatively.

"Well . . . back when I was a young girl," she said dreamily, "I did like poetry."

"Really?" I asked, barely concealing my excitement.

She snapped back to her normal stiffness. "Yes, but soon there was no time for that. I had to work to support my younger brothers and sisters. Then I got married and my husband and children kept me busy enough."

"How about now? Would you like to write poetry these days?"

"Well, I never thought about it," she replied. Then adding, with a hint of playfulness, "I suppose I do have all the time in the world on my hands."

To make a long story short, I encouraged Sue to let her "grandmother" write poetry. This meant that in the evenings, Sue "became" her grandmother: she sat like her grandmother, scrunched up her face like the old woman, and made little movements like she used to make. Then she picked up a pen and paper and wrote whatever came out. Sue was surprised to find that her "grandmother" wrote poems about love and joy, about longing for a life she had never led. Soon after, Sue told me that her muse had returned. Her painting took on a new life, and she even shifted to a new style, after having been stuck in the same routine for years.

Though she was long dead, to Sue her grandmother was living and breathing and causing a lot of mischief. Her jealousy stopped Sue from painting. "I was never able to do that, so why should anyone else?" was the inner grandmother's basic attitude.

When engaged in her own creativity, though, she had no desire to hold Sue back anymore.

Many of us have jealous inner figures. We are so full of them it is amazing they all fit in the chair when we sit down. Your father, your mother, your sister, your brother, your child, your partner, your friend, your teacher, your student, or practically anybody might be in there blocking your creativity because she or he is jealous of your potential. So do a little inner voodoo. Become that person and let her create. Who knows? You may even like her style.

Getting Help from Your Inner Critic

Nothing stops the creative flow more quickly than a sharp comment, a dismissing look, or a disdainful laugh coming from somewhere deep inside. I know—it's devastating when the criticism comes from outside, too. But outer criticism wouldn't faze us unless we agreed with it on some level. Inner critics seem to want nothing less than our complete annihilation. In actuality, though, they may have very specific goals. With this knowledge, and a little work, it is often possible to transform your critic and even get it to help you with your creativity.

Have a chat with your inner critic. You can do this on paper, or out loud, as you prefer. The first step is to bring it out of hiding. Ask your critic what it does not like about you. This may unleash a furious barrage that may be hard to listen to, but don't be discouraged. You are only priming the pump, getting your critic comfortable by asking it to talk about its favorite subject. When it starts to run out of steam, or when you've had enough, shift the topic. Ask your critic what it wants from you. This is a really important question.

Your critic might answer that it wants you to be smarter but that you are hopelessly stupid. This is a positive answer, believe it or not. It shows that your critic would actually like to improve you if it could. What does your critic want? Beauty? Truth? Clarity? Strength? Vulnerability? Humor? Of course, your critic thinks you have none of these qualities. But maybe you want these things, too. If you and your critic share even one goal, there is a bit of common ground between you. The battle is already half over. Here is one example of such an interaction.

Critic: You stupid idiot! You can't put a sentence together to save your life. Look at the way you are writing this section! It is so unclear. You might as well give up, you fool. What do you know about creativity anyway? Get a job!

Lane: What do you want from me?

Critic: From you? Nothing! From a real writer, I would expect that he write clearly and help the reader to understand the subject matter. But you are useless!

Lane: Hmmm. You are fighting for clarity. I like that, too. Maybe you could teach me.

Critic: You? Give me a break!

Lane: No, seriously. I really value your input. If you want me to write with more clarity, please help me. What is not clear here?

Critic: Well, for one thing, you haven't explained yet how to actually interact with an inner critic. You are demonstrating it with me because you don't have a clear way of telling people how to do it.

Lane: That is true. I figured it is such an individual thing, that people would just have to follow their own process as it unfolds.

Critic: If they knew how to follow their process already, they would not need to read this book, dummy! Give them more precise tools.

Lane: I'm at a loss. Maybe you could give me a hint about what type of tools you are talking about.

Critic: That's not my job. I just criticize.

Lane: Well, dear critic, I think you are not a very good critic. Instead of just standing on the sidelines and kibitzing, use your amazing clarity to help me!

Critic: OK already. I get your point. Well, that tool you just used is pretty valuable. Tell the people to *criticize their critics*. Tell them to force their critics to make the criticism more useful. Not that I liked it when you just did that, mind you.

Lane: Sorry about that, but you really are a pain in the neck when you only criticize instead of using your insights to help me. I want to co-create with you. You can be really useful. In fact, you helped me out here. Thanks.

Critic: Don't mention it, chump.

To sum up (before it comes back and yells at me because that wasn't clear enough):

1. Ask your inner critic what it does not like about you.

2. Find out your critic's goals.

3. Ask your critic to help you meet those goals.

4. Don't take "no" for an answer. (Critics are lazy. Oh, yeah, they work overtime bugging you. But try to get them to do some real work, like help you with a creative project! Then they make all kinds of excuses and say it is your job.)

5. Criticize your critic. Tell it that if it were any good at… clarity, beauty, whatever… it could tell you more specifically what to do to meet your common goals.

6. Be merciless, just like your critic is—don't give up until you have gotten the help you need.

Becoming the Block

Most people who feel blocked in their creativity or expression naturally want nothing more than to get through whatever is blocking them. As we have seen again and again, though, the thing that disturbs us is often somehow meaningful. If that is true, then the block itself might be able to teach us something.

Ewan was a participant in a seminar (that I co-led with two speech and language therapists) for people who stutter. A bear of a man, Ewan stood with hunched shoulders and a lowered head, saying quietly that something blocks his speech and expression. Every few words, the flow of conversation was stopped for seconds at a time as he struggled to get past certain consonants. He held his breath, unable to release the sound. His hands circled and moved forward in the silence, as if trying to carry on the task that his voice would not complete. Ewan described his stammer as a huge, insurmountable wall. It was impossible to get through it, he said, impossible to get around it, impossible to get over it, and impossible to get under it. He experienced speaking as a constant battle with this wall that could not be breached.

Since there was no way to fight the wall, I suggested, maybe he could become it. I asked him to show me what the wall was like. Ewan slowly straightened himself, growing to his full height. His shoulders slowly squared and his barrel chest expanded. He looked down at me and said, totally fluently and in a loud clear voice, "Don't fuck with me!" I was floored. The transformation was incredible.

Gathering my wits together, I told him that I did not like that he was always blocking me, and I wanted to get through him. He boomed, "Don't even try it. Don't mess with me," again with no trace of a stammer. I pushed against him but I felt like a gnat trying to move a mountain.

As we worked further, it became clear that Ewan needed this "wall energy" in his interactions with people. He sometimes allowed himself to be pushed around and certainly did not see himself as being powerful. But when he thought of the wall as his ally rather than his enemy—when he identified with its impenetrable strength—Ewan's expression, his speech, and his whole being changed dramatically.

What stops you from expressing yourself and creating? Don't just suffer from the feeling of being blocked, but really *study it.* How do you experience the block? Describe it in detail to a friend or on paper. Then become "the blocker," that thing that normally stops you. Take over that quality. Let your body and your feelings and your mind transform until you are completely like "the blocker." Now let that energy, that quality, create. How does it express itself? What would it create? What does it want to say? How would it interact with people and in the world? Be it. Get to know it. Learn to love it.

Creative Reactions

I can hear you protesting, "No! The block is terrible! I hate it! I don't want it! It gets me so angry and frustrated that I want to blow it up!" OK. Process work teaches us to be with what *is.* Right now, anger and frustration are present. So be angry and frustrated. Let that create.

I had done all the research for my master's thesis and it was finally time to write, but I could not type a single word. I sat there staring at the blank screen for weeks. Each day my frustration and anger mounted. Finally, I felt a huge rage boiling inside me. I wanted to smash the computer. Instead I found myself screaming curses at the top of my lungs and typing with loud vicious strokes that thankfully did not break the keyboard. I cursed my life, my parents, my fate, my school, my teachers, and especially that Godforsaken topic I was supposed to write about. Why I had ever chosen it anyway? Good %*#!ing question, I shouted back, writing in a flood of four-letter words about the idiotic thing that had interested me way back when. I wrote for hours until the venting had left me exhausted.

When I looked at it the next day, I was bored by the twenty-odd pages of repetitive outbursts. But somewhere in the middle, and then nearer to the end, were a couple of kernels of something interesting. There was the core of what I really wanted to say in my thesis. I deleted the huge majority of that tirade and was left with two paragraphs. Two paragraphs that I liked. Two paragraphs that inspired me to write more.

If you have a creative block and feel a big reaction to the block, use your reaction. Write, paint, sing, move all your feelings about the block. Get angry, sad, frustrated, or depressed and keep expressing those feelings in whatever medium you choose. Use four-letter words or obscene gestures if that's what comes. Keep going. Express the same thing again and again until you have gone through it to the other side. You will eventually get to what you want to say. Don't worry about the form or how to say it. Just start creating with whatever energy is in you. The rest will take care of itself.

Procrastinatin' Rhythm

You all know the scene. The creativity just won't flow. You're looking out the window or eating or pacing the floor or playing basketball with crumpled paper or biting your nails or doing any number of inane and time-wasting activities. If you start to value and unfold what is actually happening, though, doing "nothing" will soon become more interesting than you might think.

Do you stare out the window? Then really look. Notice what catches your attention out there. Is it a bird flying? A tree? The wind? A car? A person? Now become whatever catches your attention. Don't think of it as something separate from yourself. It is "flirting" with you in this moment because your creativity needs it. Move like it, make sounds like it. Feel it all through your body. What quality does it have? Notice how it is different from the normal "you." Go deeper into it now. Go back to that movement and that sound and that feeling. Do it with every part of your body. Even your toes. And your face. Now let it take over your mind. Even your breathing. Now let that create.

Or do you pace around your home or studio? Then really pace and notice the energy and quality of your walking. Do you make sharp turns? Sudden stops? Drag your feet on the ground? Almost lose your balance? Feel rigid? Slouch? Look straight ahead? Meander? Exaggerate the unusual aspect of your walk (whichever part feels strange or out of the ordinary or catches your attention). Keep exaggerating it. Let it move the way it wants to, without losing that original quality that caught your attention.

Now ask yourself, who or what moves like this? Don't be satisfied by the answer, "That's me." Go back to the movement and ask again. Maybe it is a person, or maybe an animal or a spirit or a creature from a fairy tale. Let that figure create what it wants to create. If you can't think of someone or something, just keep moving in this way until you feel the energy or quality of this movement with every fiber of your being. Now let this energy or quality create. Or let your mind/brush/voice/instrument/character/etc. drag around or leap around or goose step or spin or somehow use whatever energy you discovered.

These techniques will bring you into a different state of consciousness, a different mindset. The important thing to remember is that this new state or mindset was trying to happen already. It was inherent in your gazing out the window or pacing the floor or whatever you were doing. Don't resist it. Follow it. Let it create. What do you have to lose? It can't be more of a waste of time than what you were doing before.

Distraction

One of creativity's biggest enemies is distraction. You are trying to focus on one thing, but something else grabs your attention for a moment, until the next thing pulls you away even from that diversion. There might be something important about whatever is distracting you. Or maybe the process of distraction itself can be your meditation object.

One day, while trying to prepare a seminar, I was particularly distracted. My mind rushed from one thought to the next, with no hope of focusing on "the topic." I couldn't think straight and was certainly getting no work done, so I decided to focus on my lack of focus. I noticed that my mind worked in a strange way. It made quick and seemingly irrational associations, connecting words because they sounded similar. Or two different meanings of a single word were somehow joined in the mixed-up jumble of my distraction. This all happened so quickly that the end of one idea dovetailed into the beginning of another. No wonder I couldn't finish a single sentence. So I wrote the following song, using the same dovetailing associations to describe the process that was happening at lightning speed in my scattered brain.

> *Thousand flashes of light bounce through my*
> *head—games plotting revenge, regrets,*
> *remorses screaming what should, what could, what*
> *mighty forces disturb my peaceful*
> *restive hordes debating when to*
> *striking out when threatened by the*
> *enemies perceived, real, or*
> *imagine life without this constant fight.*
>
> *Hungry ghosts demanding to be*
> *fed up with the style of life where*
> *one thing isn't finished before the*
> *next in line please move at a faster*
> *pace the floor don't ever settle*

> *downward spirals searching for the*
> *grounded by the parents in your*
> *mindfulness is just a breath away.*

> *It's so easy to*
> *forgetfulness is just a way of*
> *lifetimes spent without*
> *awareness is a word I think I*
> *herds of lemming—thoughts.*

Once my lemming thoughts had followed one another over the cliff and into the sea, my brain settled down and I could get back to work. But the seminar preparation was not half as interesting, nor half as fun, as focusing on my distraction and writing that song.

How do you get distracted? Does one thought or feeling keep attracting your attention, like the inexorable pull of a whirlpool? Stop resisting and instead *investigate* it. Maybe that thought or feeling wants to create. Or study the process of distraction itself. Notice the speed of your brain as it flits from one idea to the next. Use that same speed in your creativity. Discover the quality of your distracted mind, whatever it is, and use that to create with.

Somebody Say Amen

The biggest block is often our own attitude toward our creativity. We don't believe in whatever is trying to come through us. We judge it or don't pay attention to it. We may think, "This is not the right moment, I'm in the middle of something else," or "I don't want to create that. That's stupid." By trying to control our creativity, we forget to pay attention to how it is already emerging. In such moments, it may be helpful to remember gospel music.

Some might think it strange that a Jewish boy from New York could love gospel music so much. But I adore the passion, the soulfulness, the hallowed hush, and the ecstatic wail. I love how feelings, rising up from somewhere deep inside the singers, change the song from moment to moment. This is also true in the rest of the service. I remember a certain church that had soul-stirring music on Sunday mornings. The ushers gave each member of the congregation a sheet of paper listing the order of prayers, hymns, etc. At the bottom of the page was written, "Program subject to change due to the controlling influence of the Holy Spirit." And they kept to their word.

One week, as the preacher was giving his sermon, a man started talking loudly in the pews. Then he stood up and kept talking. I couldn't understand what he was saying, and thought he was a homeless person or someone in an extreme state of consciousness. I expected the ushers to come and gently escort him out of the church. But that did not happen. Instead, the preacher and the congregation waited patiently. Eventually the man finished speaking and sat down. The preacher said, "Amen, brother; thank you," and spoke about the importance of listening when the Spirit rises in us. Then he went on with his sermon. That openness to what was happening in the moment—the acceptance of this man who was moved to speak, even in the middle of the sermon—really impressed me. That same acceptance and freedom permeates the gospel music I love.

We could use a healthy dollop of that attitude when approaching our creativity. When inspiration comes, our challenge is to open up to it, to believe it is a divine spark expressing itself through us. No matter what bubbles up, we need to learn to love and appreciate it. No matter how strange it may seem or how much it seems to go against what we had intended to say or create, we should honor it by at least hearing it out, by finding out what it has to say or wants to create. By saying "Amen" to it.

Where I grew up, when someone sang, you listened until the end of the song and then applauded. When someone sings gospel, though, the congregation doesn't wait to voice their support. One of my favorite recordings is "Somebody's Knocking, Part II" from the album "Having Church" by Reverend James Cleveland and the Southern California Community Choir. Piano and organ start it off quietly, slowly. A woman from the choir shouts, "Thank you, Lord!" Another, "Hallelujah!" Then, as bass and drums join the other instruments, Wayne Anthony, an amazing vocalist, starts his solo.

In a soft, clear voice he sings, "Somebody's knocking at your door." Before he even finishes this first line, someone says, "Oh yeah" and others chime in, "Come on, Wayne!" With a tone rich and full of feeling, Wayne implores, "Why, why, why, why, why, why don't you answer?" A man echoes, "Why? Why?" Wayne starts to turn the melody inside out, building, rising, his voice getting bluesier and more powerful. The band is building, too, the back-beat driving, the music supporting the singer, carrying him. The choir's encouragement also builds. Shouting praise, they egg him on. "Alright! Sing! Hallelujah! Sing it, Wayne! Yeah!" Wayne changes the tune completely, leaving the constraints of the original melody. The piano echoes this new bluesy melody a moment after he sings it. Shouts ring out, "Go, Wayne! Thank you, Lord! Sing, Wayne!"

The song peaks in long, fervent, high notes, a heart-wrenching plea. The choir, the band, it seems the air itself, is supporting this awesome singer, echoing him, loving him, praising him, somehow joining his song while still letting him sing it alone. In my living room I'm laughing, screaming, crying. Not only because his singing fills my heart to the bursting point. Not only because the song reminds me to open up whenever the divine knocks at my door. But also because I love listening to a community that supports its members in their deepest expression, their most passionate creativity, and their most honest spirituality.

We all need that. Creating can be a lonely business. But we can support each other as a community dedicated to creativity. Ask your friends how their creative projects are coming along. Praise their efforts and celebrate their breakthroughs. Commiserate in their blocks or, even better, help them to find whatever is trying to express itself through their blocks. Form a "creativity choir" that loves each soloist. Build a community that accepts strange outbursts, that values unexpected howling, that says Amen to all of its members. Forge a pot in which you can all cook your creative juices, a pot that is happy when the unknown, the divine, bubbles to the surface.

Try This:

This chapter is already filled with exercises. Try them all. And then create a group dedicated to supporting one another's creativity. Meet once a week, or once a month, and talk about your successes and failures. Show each other your work. Read to one another. Sing praises, shout support. Help each other to find and support the unintentional parts of what you are creating. Work on your jealousy of one another. Help each other to interact with inner critics. Practice the exercises in this chapter, and the other exercises in this book, translating them to fit whatever medium you are working with. Enjoy!

Chapter 13

Creative Intent

This book has sung the praises of the unintentional. But what about *intention?* Does it have no importance in this creative universe? Are we supposed to just float around, buffeted by the winds of chance, following one unintentional signal after the next, with no will of our own? Must our creativity and our lives be totally dependent on what happens to us and not at all driven by what we like and what we want?

I've been teaching and writing about the unintentional for many years. I love it, use it, identify with it. Whoops! Sounds like a primary process to me! If I'm so attached to the unintentional, then intention itself must be outside of my box. How exciting! This gives me a chance to step outside of my normal identity. Without further ado, let's take a foray into the wild and wonderful world of intention and its relationship to creativity and life.

Hurray for Intention!

It is marvelous to make choices, saying yes to this and no to that. I love this person. I don't want to spend my life with that one. I want this job. That one would bore me. I love this song so I will sing it. It doesn't sound good to me yet, so I will practice until it does. Mmmm, that's what I like. That's what I want. What a pleasure!

We need intention. Our creativity needs it. An intention to play Beethoven will lead us to practice scales. An intention to master figure drawing will lead us to study anatomy and to seek out a good art class. An intention to perform will send us to one audition after the next. An intention to have a garden will get us down on our hands and knees pulling weeds. Without intention we would never make the sacrifices necessary to pursue our art. Without intention we would lack the discipline it takes to realize our dreams.

Other aspects of intention are also important to the creative process. You may have an intention, for instance, to convey something through your creativity, to express a feeling or an idea. You may intend to have a certain effect on an audience. Why, for instance, does someone create a garden? Does she want to create something beautiful? Or eat the vegetables? Or bring joy to the people passing by? Does she feel nurtured when she nurtures her plants?

When you are creating, it can sometimes be useful to ask yourself the following questions: What do you want to convey? What effect do you want to have (on yourself or on someone else)? What do you hope to achieve? What is your course of action? How will you reach your desired goals?

Of course, creativity is not always so well thought out. My motivation for writing songs is very rarely a desire to communicate something or have an effect. It's rather that I feel that something inside of me needs to come out. My intention then, if I examine it, is to give voice to an otherwise inexpressible emotion. I may be unaware of my intention at the time, but it is there nonetheless. When writing this book, however, I have very specific, conscious goals, very clear messages I want to convey. I do want to have an effect on you, dear reader. And it is my intention to use certain tools—clarity, examples, a relaxed tone, etc.—to the best of my ability in order to achieve my aim.

Deadly Intent

Sometimes problems help us to focus our intention. Last winter, I was not feeling well. I went to a well-respected practitioner of Chinese medicine who scared the daylights out of me. After examining me and taking my pulse, he asked me if there was a history of liver problems in my family. When I said I did not know of any, he replied that sometimes people die of cancer and do not know the cause. After yelling at him for being so dramatic and alarming, I went home and meditated on my death. He had not said I would die, but I guess I have a bit of Woody Allen in me.

I asked myself, if I die in one year, what would be important for me to achieve? Would I need to build my private practice in the San Francisco Bay Area? (I had just moved here from Poland a few months earlier.) No, if I had only one year to live, then building a practice would not be important. Would I need lots of students? Also not.

What, then, would I want to do in that hypothetical last year? I felt that the most important thing in my life would be to try to publish this book. I had already written it, but had stalled at the point of trying to sell it. Once I realized that this was vitally important to me, I decided to spend all of my time and energy on that task. And within three months of focus and hard work, I found a publisher. My liver turned out to be fine, and my symptoms went away. (Probably it didn't hurt that I changed my diet after the doctor scared me.) Now I am spending the summer doing final revisions. Sometimes new clients call. It is sorely tempting to increase my income and get my professional feet on the ground in my new home. Then I remember my death. Even though it very likely will not come for many years, my death reminds me that this creative project is the most important part of my life right now. So I politely ask the clients to call back at the end of the summer.

Part of intention means setting boundaries, so I jealously guard the time I need with my book. I am thankful to those symptoms (the Tao expressing itself through my body) and that doctor, for getting me in touch with what was most important to me. They helped me to set priorities and focus on my core, creative intention above all else.

Pit Bull Intent

I hate pit bulls. It is very rare for me to hate something, especially an animal. But I truly hate pit bulls. For those of you who don't know, a pit bull is a kind of dog that was bred for fighting. It has a strange jaw that locks when it bites, so it cannot release its hold. (I'll probably get hate mail from pit bull owners. I'm sure your particular dog is lovely.)

Being a process worker, I was puzzled by my aversion to these creatures and tried to discover the pit bull in me, and how it might be useful in my life. I realized that I need to be like a pit bull in certain situations. I need to bite down on something and not let go, no matter what. One of those situations is when I am in the middle of a creative project. Then I need the pit bull energy, to sink my teeth into what I am working on and not let go until it is complete. This is a kind of intention. I call it "pit bull intent." The dogs still bug me. But I love pit bull intent.

But wait, you might think. The last chapter said that we should follow our distractions. If we have pit bull intent, then aren't we ignoring the things that distract and disturb us? Ah, yes. But sometimes it is important to ignore distractions and disturbances, if they get in the way of what we are trying to create. If someone calls when I'm in the middle of a paragraph, for instance, there is no way I will follow that distraction. The pit bull just growls at the phone as I sink my teeth into whatever I'm writing. But if I make the choice to focus on something that distracts and disturbs me, I do that like a pit bull, too. In the last chapter, I described how I followed my distraction. I grabbed onto my wandering mind with pit bull awareness. I let my thinking twist and turn and scramble to get away, but the teeth of my awareness never let it go for an instant. I didn't open my jaws until it had yielded me a song. Then I licked my chops and went on with my original task.

Elephant Intent

It's only fair to balance that last section with a discussion of my favorite animal, the elephant. I never thought about elephants much until they started appearing regularly in my dreams over the years. Elephants guide me on my path. Whenever I wonder which way to go, the elephant tells me, "Come with me." When I ask where we are going, he replies, "As long as you are with me, you are on the right path." The elephant is, for me, a process guide. Elephant intent, for me, is the intention to follow the process. Slowly. One step at a time. I'd like to tell a story about following the elephant. It is not about creativity per se, but rather about intending to follow the unintentional in life.

I lived in Poland for four-and-a-half years. I loved it there. My music thrived, my creativity blossomed, my work deepened and was appreciated. But I felt it was not the place to spend my life. So I waited for a dream to tell me where to live, where to grow roots. It might seem like a strange way to make such a big decision. But for me, that was the only way. I wanted guidance from something other than my normal consciousness. I waited for two years. That was a long time. But I held my intention to wait for a sign from the unintentional. I finally had the following dream.

I was looking at an apartment to rent. It was on the ground floor of a building, and one entire wall was covered with windows,

*from floor to ceiling. Out the windows, I could see the water in the
distance. I was surprised I could see the water, since the apartment
was on the ground floor. I liked the apartment very much.*

I woke up happy, but without knowing where the apartment
was. I held my intention. A few days later, I had another dream.

*I was looking at an apartment to rent. Again, there was a
whole wall of windows. Again, I could see the water. It was in the
San Francisco Bay area.*

I made a decision to move to the San Francisco Bay area. (I
realize how lucky I am to be able to move freely around the
planet!) I arrived and started apartment hunting immediately. It
was nearly impossible to find a place. All the apartments were
incredibly overpriced, and most of those available were unappe-
tizing, with windows that looked out at walls a few feet away. After
a long and unsuccessful search, I finally found an apartment that
was pretty nice. I begged the landlord to take me. He said he
would need a week to check my references. I begged him to do it
faster. He said he'd try. I went back to the seedy hotel where I was
staying and had a strange dream.

*I saw a man with the head of an elephant. The elephant head
got smaller and smaller until it was the head of a rabbit. Then the
leash that had been around his neck slipped off, because his head
was so much smaller than it had been. At the same moment, I heard
the sentence: "Don't let the elephant's head shrink down to a rabbit's head or the leash will fall off."*

Remember, elephants have always taught me to take one slow
step after another, and to trust that I am on the right track if I am
with them. A rabbit, on the other hand, is scared and jumps into the
first hole he can find. I realized that if I let my elephant head (the
one who trusts the process and stays on the path without knowing
the ultimate goal) shrink into a rabbit head (the one who is scared
and wants a quick solution), then the leash would fall off. That
would mean that I would not be led by something bigger than I am.

At the precise moment that I understood the meaning of my dream, the phone rang. The landlord had checked my references and I could move in immediately. I took a breath and told him this was too fast for me, that I needed more time. He thought I was crazy, since I had just begged him to decide as quickly as possible. He told me I would lose the apartment if he found someone else. The rabbit was shaking with fear, but I heard the elephant say that I needed more time anyway. I was going on faith. Faith in the process. Faith in my dreams. I was following my intention to follow the unintentional. I got down on my knees and prayed to Ganesh, the Hindu god with the body of a man and the head of an elephant, and drove off to the apartment-hunting service to pick up the day's listing of offerings.

I parked across from the office, and happened to notice a store that sells things from India. It was just opening its doors. I bought a small statue of Ganesh and put it in my pocket. When I got the list of available apartments one caught my eye immediately. I called and a woman answered and told me to come right over. A few minutes later I arrived at a big apartment building in Oakland. I was hoping the apartment was on one of the top floors, dreading yet another view of a concrete wall. So when the landlady put her key in a door on the ground floor, I was disappointed. Until the door opened. A whole wall was filled with windows from floor to ceiling, and I could see water (the San Francisco Bay) in the distance. This was exactly like my dream! I was surprised to be able to see the water from the ground floor but then realized that the building was at the top of a hill. Before even looking around, I said, "I'll take it." She said, "You haven't even seen the apartment yet." I looked, then told her I had made up my mind. The landlady took my references and told me to come back the following morning. I walked out to the street, put the statue of Ganesh on the sidewalk, and bowed deeply. The next day, the apartment was mine.

It took faith—a faith I don't always have—for me to follow my dreams like that. It took a firm intention to follow something irrational, to follow a process that was not under my conscious control. I am not a Hindu. When the dream showed me my old friend the elephant with the body of a man, though, I recognized Ganesh, and bowed to this manifestation of my dreaming process. He reminded me of my commitment to be led by something, to follow the path without knowing the result. And Ganesh, the remover of all obstacles, led me to the apartment of my dreams. I sit here now, at three in the morning, writing. I am home.

The Dynamic Interplay of Intention and the Unintentional

The unintentional appears at the moment when something ineffable is trying to express itself through us. You might call that something Nature or the Tao or the dreaming process. Perhaps you call it Spirit or God or the Goddess or a Higher Power. Maybe you prefer to think of it as the irrational or the unconscious or the numinous or the mystery or the unknown. Or you could be more at ease calling it your deepest self or your original nature or the ground of being, or the pattern inherent in the chaos. You can use whatever name fits your belief system.

I grew up in an atheist Jewish household. My parents' basic feeling was that there is no God, and if there is, he is a jerk. Otherwise, how could the Holocaust have happened? In college, I loved to write papers for my philosophy of religion class proving that God does not exist. Camus convinced me I could never be sure one way or the other, so I became an agnostic. When I encountered process work, though, I had experiences of something other than me, bigger than me, wiser than me.

My work with others and my own personal work have caused my jaw to drop again and again, leaving me in awe of the power and beauty of whatever is out there. I don't know what to call it. I feel most comfortable describing it as the dreaming process or Nature or the Tao. Those names fit best for me. I truly think it is impossible to name. Experience has taught me, though, that something *is* trying to happen. Whatever that something is, it can have a profound effect on our music, our creativity, and our lives.

Many spiritual traditions recommend giving up your will to God, following the Tao, surrendering to something greater than yourself. Intention, though, plays a role here as well. You choose to follow this path. You want it. You must hold this intention in the face of all the internal and external pressures to lead a "normal life." There is a paradox here. To follow the unintentional, you have to make a decision, a commitment. You have to hold onto your intention to not simply follow your own intentions.

The creative process, like life, is a dynamic interplay between what we want and what happens to us. I woke up this morning with ideas for this chapter. Lying there in bed, I let the words drift into my consciousness and then wrote them in my dream journal. But they stopped. So I lay there waiting, in a half-dreaming state, opening a space in case more thoughts would come. Once I had created a space for them, they did appear. The ideas just happened to me. I could not force that process. (I know, because I tried all day yesterday and it didn't work!) They came without my effort, unintentionally. My intention to create a space for them, though, gave them enough time to percolate.

Those few words in my journal were like unformed clay, the raw material of the creative process. Now it is up to me to mold them, to use my will and my craft in order to give them shape. It is my intention, in this moment, to make them accessible and understandable. And so the dance continues, until the next unintentional thing happens to block my way or give me inspiration.

We are co-creators of our music, our art, and our creative projects. We cannot take full responsibility for our inspirations, nor must we give full credit to the muse. We can only have an intention to hold a space for the spirit of creativity, then wait for something—a sound, a movement, a word, an idea, a feeling, a hunch, a shape, a quality of light—to rise from the depths and meet us. Then we must step into the creation with our intention, make our unique imprint on it, give it form and life. The unintentional helps us to find what is still unexpressed and to discover how it wants to be expressed. It is ultimately up to us, though, to have the intention, the discipline, and the courage to express it.

Try This:

Four Meditations on Intent

1. Deadly Intent: If you had one year to live, what creative project would you want to accomplish? Discover what is most important to you, about your life, and about your creativity.

2. Pit Bull Intent: Carve time out of your day (and your week, and your month, and your year) so that you make sure to really give yourself enough space to accomplish the answer to #1. Make a promise to yourself to do this, and growl at anything that gets in your way. During those times, sink your teeth into your creative project and *do not let go.*

3. Creative Intent: When you are working on a creative project, ask yourself these questions:
   What do you want to convey?
   What effect do you want to have (on yourself or on someone else)?
   What do you hope to achieve?
   How will you reach your desired goals?

4. Elephant Intent: How committed are you to following the process if something unintentional comes up that challenges your answers to number three? Do you have any helpers (in real life or in your dreams) who can guide you? You can use other exercises in this book—particularly from the following chapter—to find inner guides.

Chapter 14

Co-Creation:
The Awesome Interplay of Art and Life

But What If...

Saying yes to what happens can sometimes be challenging. In order to come into contact with the dreaming process, we often have to look beyond our intentions, beyond our identities, and embrace precisely those things that we hate, that we fear, that we would prefer to forget or ignore. The Tao is not just a nice word. It does not only express itself in musical mistakes and unintended brush strokes. Sometimes it shakes the very foundations of our existence. Sometimes it scares us out of our wits.

What if, for instance, we intend to live, and the unintentional comes as a life-threatening illness? What if we intend to create, and our bodies no longer permit us to hold the tools of our trade? Will we still have the courage, the will, to follow what happens? Will we still step into the dreaming process, even if it seems to be leading us away from what we hold dearest in our hearts?

A musical mistake, repeated and exaggerated, seems to lead us ever further from the music we want to create. If we suspend judgment, though, and continue to follow the dreaming process, we can discover music and meaning beyond our imagination. When an experience threatens our way of creating, our way of life, or even our very life itself, we naturally fear that we may be pulled toward our worst nightmare. But that nightmare, that terrifying experience, when unfolded and appreciated, may in fact have the potential to transform our lives, and our creativity, at the deepest level.

A year ago, sick with cancer and unable to do the artistic work she had always loved, my mom was left facing death or a life she felt was not worth living. Especially in such moments, it is hard to trust what is happening. How could she follow what *is*, when it seemed only horrendous and destructive? I had the incredible privilege to witness her transform the ultimate creative block into a new creative opportunity, the worst irreparable scratch into a magnificent rose. Her story remains extraordinary to me.

The Ultimate Creative Block

My mom was diagnosed with blood cancer about a year ago. Even though there had been no big symptoms and the doctors had not been able to find anything wrong with her, she had known for a while that something was terribly wrong. She had even pressured my father to complete their estate planning, although she had had no reason to believe there was any rush. Somehow, she had known.

More than a year before her diagnosis, I was walking with my mom in the Pepsico Sculpture Gardens in Purchase, New York. She was tired and out of breath, which I thought was strange since she was usually so active and vibrant. We had been looking at a trio of Native American totem poles when she became very sad and confided in me that she had recently been unable to sculpt. My mom has been a professional sculptor for most of her adult life. She loves carving stone and wood, and is always thrilled to be in her studio, covered with stone dust or wood chips. For some reason, though, she had not been working lately. Whenever she tried, she felt tired. She was sure it was a creative block, a physical manifestation of something going on in her head. Since this was my specialty, she said, maybe I could help her. I was so touched that she asked me. We had long ago worked through our difficulties, and our relationship was very close. But this felt like a new shift, with her seeing me as a professional and as a friend, not just as a son.

Although we were surrounded by beautiful art, the atmosphere was sad and heavy. I asked her what happened when she tried to sculpt. She said that she had no energy and felt slightly depressed. Nothing inspired her. I asked what else was going on in her life that might be getting her down. She stopped walking and looked at me as if she was trying to make a decision. Then she took a deep breath and told me about an incident a few months earlier when she had had short memory lapses. They had only happened a few times, but they scared her terribly.

When I asked what was so frightening, she said that she was afraid she would lose her intellect, her rationality. After recommending that she see a doctor to check it out medically, I suggested that she might also try to *lose her intellect on purpose* once in a while. (I was thinking that this symptom might be trying to teach her something. She had always been very rational. Turning off her mind for a moment could be a good practice for her.) She had a very strong reaction against this idea.

"My intellect *is me*," she said. "That's who I am. I'm afraid to lose the kernel of myself." My mom started to cry. She said she felt something terrible was happening to her. There was no rational evidence for it, but she could not shake the feeling. Her worst fear, she said, was that she would become a drag on her husband, my father. She was afraid to lose him, or to make his life miserable. I was so touched by her love for him. I suggested that she make a sculpture about her love, about her passion. She had often sculpted mothers and children, women playing, or women trans-forming into birds. But I had never seen her create a piece about a man and a woman. Maybe it was time for that. And, I went on, if her tiredness did not allow her to work in stone or wood, maybe she could write love poetry. This last suggestion, she told me much later, planted a seed that would bloom in unexpected ways.

Walking Away from Your Own Funeral

Her diagnosis was, of course, a shock and a horror to the whole family. One of the worst things about it for my mom was that her doctor forbade her to sculpt. The cancer in her blood caused edemas, bleeding under her skin. Since carving involves a lot of banging, the doctor was afraid that the resulting trauma might start internal bleeding that would not stop. So she was not allowed to work even when she was not feeling so weak. When she was begin-ning her chemotherapy, she called me on the phone and told me the following short dream.

I am at my own funeral. I see myself, dead, wrapped in "swad-dling clothes."

My mom was very depressed. The moment to die might be nearing, she thought. She had decided she did not want to be kept alive at all costs. Her feeling was that a life of suffering and further and further weakness, consisting only of one treatment after another, was not a life worth living. The dream seemed to confirm her worst fears, and contributed to her feeling of hopelessness and surrender.

When we talked about her dream, though, another point of view began to emerge. I asked her about swaddling clothes. She said that this is the shroud that was used to wrap corpses back in the Old Country. Her father (who was born in a shtetl in Poland) used to tell her that this was how people were buried there. I mentioned that I had always thought of swaddling clothes as what babies were wrapped in. She was very embarrassed, saying that this was true, that she had used the wrong word. But, she said in a confused tone, in the dream it was definitely called *swaddling clothes*. It was a burial shroud but, for some reason, was called by that other name. Things were getting more interesting and mysterious, but not yet understandable.

I asked my mom what her father had told her about those shrouds. He had grown up in an orthodox Jewish home. (His father had been a rabbi, all his brothers had been rabbis, and all his sisters had married rabbis.) He had told her that in the Old Country, Jews wrapped their dead in sheets so that, when the Messiah came, it would be easy for them to get up out of the grave. If they were locked in caskets, then they would not be able to emerge. This was fascinating to me, especially since her dream had replaced the word "shroud" or "sheets" with "swaddling clothes." Newborn babies are wrapped in swaddling clothes, and the shroud is worn in order to facilitate rebirth. Her dream's wordplay was turning out to be more and more meaningful.

I asked my mom what she thought of the Messiah and the idea of life after death. She said that she had never believed in that stuff. Wondering whether maybe, facing death, she could be reevaluating her beliefs, I asked how she felt about it these days. She repeated that all that religious stuff did nothing for her. This was obviously not the right direction, so I tried a different tack. I said that her dream showed her dead, but dressed in swaddling clothes like a baby at the beginning of life, or in a sheet like someone who was expecting to be reborn. Maybe, I suggested, her dream was saying that she needed to "come back to life" now. Instead of giving into the depression and just waiting to die, it might be time to get up and live. The moment I said these words, her mood seemed to change.

She said, yes, that felt really right. She started to talk about going to the theatre and doing other things that made her feel alive. She said she was very tired from the chemotherapy and might not be able to do as much as she would like to do. But she needed to step back into life and not just act like she was dead already. She realized that she truly had been watching her own funeral by watching herself lie down and give up. It was time to live, she decided, even if she only had a short time left.

There was one big problem, though. She was forbidden to sculpt. How could she live happily, she asked, if she could not create? Then it dawned on her. Maybe she could take a writing class. It had been in the back of her mind since our talk at the sculpture garden. She had been unable to start, she now realized, because she had been grieving over the fact that she could not carve. Years earlier she had written short stories, but had stopped when it had become difficult to decide whether to spend her time writing or in the studio carving. She would try it again, she decided, since her chosen medium was closed to her. If there was still time to live, she must create.

The writing class turned out to be just what the doctor ordered. Her teacher and the other students were brought alternately to tears or laughter by the stories she read aloud each week. She found herself writing about her family, about stories she had heard since she was a girl, stories of the Old Country and the New World. The vignettes were written from different perspectives, told in the voice of her mother, or her father, or her grandmother, or herself. These short pieces seemed to fit together, and she had fantasies of joining them into a book. But she got stuck.

She had no idea which of the stories she had heard were true and which were lies. Her mother and grandmother had always fabricated stories and stretched the truth beyond recognition. Passports and birth certificates had been altered to make the holder appear younger than she was. The same story was told differently by different people, and even changed depending on the occasion or the listener. Dates were always omitted; places seemed interchangeable. It was clear, for instance, that my great grandmother had left her husband, the colonel, during some war. But which war? And which army was he actually in? It was hard to say for sure. How could she then, my mother thought, write a book when it was impossible to tell fact from fiction? The pen seemed to dry out in her hand.

Deep Rumbling

Around this time my mom and I were having lunch in Manhattan. We had just left her oncologist and were on our way to a museum, but we stopped for a bite to eat and to get out of the bitter cold. She told me about the problem she was having with her writing. I was curious whether she remembered any dreams that she had had as a girl. As we saw in chapter 4, childhood dreams often show long-term, mythic patterns that shape and influence our lives. These same patterns, Mindell discovered, can be found in our chronic or life-threatening physical symptoms.

In other words, our most frightening body problems are mirrored in our childhood dreams, and both point the way to our life myth. Maybe we could find the connection between her dream and her cancer. And maybe the myth that linked these two seemingly unrelated phenomena would be a key that could unlock her creative block. My mom said that she had had this dream repeatedly as a girl.

There is a huge pile of hollow cylindrical tubes, like big sewer pipes, on top of a hill. They are piled in a geometric pattern, with many on the bottom, fewer in the next row, etc., so they do not roll away. I hear a deep rumbling. The noise is so loud, but it assaults my inside more than it assaults my ears. I feel it in my belly. It is more upsetting to my whole inner being than it is to my ears. I know that the tubes will start to move, even though they do not look like they are going to move, and I start running away in terror. When I am part way down the hill, the pile comes loose and starts rolling after me.

I asked her which part of the dream scared her the most. (As you may remember from chapter 4, the most frightening part of our childhood dream represents our ally, an awesome spirit or energy that plagues and terrifies us but can potentially help us and guide us through life.) I thought she would surely say that the rolling tubes were the most terrifying. So I was surprised to hear that the worst thing of all was the rumbling she had heard before anything bad had happened. I asked her again, just to make sure. She repeated that that rumbling, and the fact that she knew something horrible was going to happen before there was any other proof, was unbearable.

I gently suggested that she listen to that rumbling in her imagination and feel that same sense of knowing. She closed her eyes and shuddered as I watched from across the table. I asked whether she had known that experience at any other time in her life. Her eyes opened wide and the stories started to flow. There was the time, as a little girl, when her mother had taken her away from her beloved father to live in Mexico with her grandmother. Somehow, before anyone had told her what was going to happen, she had had this same sense of foreboding and dread. There had been many such instances, she realized. She had never thought about that before. Somehow she just knew things. She had never identified with it, but it seemed to have happened over and over. She shuddered again, and told me that she had had this same sense long before her cancer diagnosis. She had just known.

This was very strange to my mom. She identified herself as a very rational woman. (She had said, "My intellect *is me*. That is who I am.") Anything spiritual or connected with the irrational was not something she usually took seriously. Yet she could not shake the reality of this experience repeating itself throughout her life. She had always, somehow, known things that she didn't even know she knew.

She was reminded of our conversation in the sculpture garden. Back then she had been scared by memory lapses (which she now was sure were connected to her as yet undiagnosed cancer).These lapses had made her afraid that she would her lose her intellect. It seemed that her illness itself was forcing her to rely on something other than her thinking. It was still hard for her, though, to believe in that strange sense of knowing in her gut.

This was a thread running through her past and her present. It was an aspect of her life myth, the deeper story that patterned her history.The rumbling that had been so terrifying in the dream was actually her ally. It told her things, important things, that no one else could tell her. This ally was scary not only because it whispered to her of painful events, but also because it threatened her cherished view of herself as being rational.

Our lunch came.As we ate she told me that she now realized that this same knowing had actually helped her to sculpt for years. It had helped her to follow the grain of the wood, to know which form was trapped inside the stone, to feel what new inspiration was lurking just beyond her consciousness. She had never thought of it in those terms before. But her creative impulse had a similar quality to that strange rumbling. She guessed that it was easier for her to follow that irrational impulse with something physical, than to do it with her head. She said,"I would get into a Zen state while sculpting, where it had nothing to do with what I was thinking. It was easier to allow that inner part of me to be in control, because it was not something I had to be rational about."

By working with her worst childhood nightmare, we had discovered an essential part of her creativity.The same rumbling that had terrified her as a girl, the same inner sense that had known about her cancer long before the doctors knew, the same irrationality that her illness itself seemed to be pushing her toward, that same mysterious something, had been helping her to sculpt for years.What had seemed to be only destructive and threatening was turning out to be connected with her deepest creative impulse.

My mom had said that it was easy to follow that inner sense when working in the physical world of stone and wood. She did not need to use her mind there. The question now was whether she could use this same creative energy with her writing, a non-physical medium that seemed to require thought.

As we waited for dessert, I asked my mom how she might use this rumbling/knowing to help her with the trouble she was having with her book. She sat silently for a long time. The big problem, she said, was that she didn't know which stories were true and which were fabricated. But that was a dilemma only for her rational mind. The rumbling would say that there is a truth that is deeper than fact. It would not worry about objective reality but instead write from a place of inner knowing. It also made sense, from the point of view of the rumbling, that each vignette was written from the perspective of a specific character. Even if the stories contradicted one another, each one was true and real for that character.

A week later, back in California, a large manila envelope appeared in my mailbox. It contained the first chapters of my mom's book. On the top of the pile was the prologue, which was written a few days after our lunch together. With her permission, I'd like to share it with you.

"I lie on my belly, on an examining table too short for my legs which uncomfortably rest on nothing but air, while large fingers push and probe above my buttocks to try to find the right bone hiding beneath my flesh. Ah, there… A long needle pierces my flesh, giving pain while trying to numb me. A wait. And then the longer hollow needle enters just there, causing a sharp pain, like an electric shock which makes my right leg jump upwards. A deeper, dull ache as the needle enters the bone. And then the aspiration of the marrow causes me to shut my eyes more tightly, anticipating that other pain, breaking off small pieces of reddened lace which I then hear placed into a vial. The marrow of my being is what they want to check.

"But the true marrow of my life is memory. My memories are only partly real. Others are recalled in a fog, are somewhat imagined because those who told me the tales upon which these rudimentary memories are based, told them from different perspectives, each being sure to make himself the hero, or else the victim.

"Weeks after my bone marrow test, when I am supposed to be getting the results, I often hear that they are inconclusive. Life, too, seems inconclusive even after I dig up and then examine the lore that forms me. And just as my red blood cells or white blood cells rise and fall at times with no apparent reason, my opinion about those who were around me varies depending upon which story I have excavated.

"I have found that there are few facts—very few firm names and dates in my history. I have made up a name or two when it is missing, have decided on a year. And yet there is a truth. . . . As myth can be more honest, more laser-like than history, so these myths mixed with reality have come to explain my inner being. With that in mind, here are my stories."

My mom is still writing her book, still reading each chapter at her writing class, still sending me installments like the serialized books that used to be published weekly in the Jewish press. She even sent me a story about my dad, a veritable love poem that still gives me goose bumps. Her chemotherapy stopped working a few months ago, so they put her on a different protocol. The side effects are maddening. But she is living. Not just alive, but living.

She walked away from her own funeral and into life, into creativity. She is terribly sad to pass by her studio every day. The stone dust still calls to her. But she has rolled with the wave that had threatened to annihilate her. Her writing, and the people who love her, have given her a reason to live. The knowing still rumbles inside of her, but it no longer frightens her. Now she uses it, creates with it. The same mysterious energy that helped to form the story of her life, she now harnesses and uses for her writing. All she had to do was to become aware of it, and to realize that it was not try-ing to kill her. No, it was offering her a gift. A gift of knowing, of mythical truth beyond fact, of depth, of creativity, of life.

Most of us have our own secret terror that we shrink from in the night. It may be an illness, or fear of illness, or an extreme state of consciousness that plagues us. It may be a dream or fantasy from childhood, or one that still makes us afraid to turn off the light. It may be relationship trouble that never seems to change, or a world problem that keeps our eyes glued to the newspaper. Perhaps you're not afraid, but all of us have something there—is it inside or outside?—that is different from us, that threatens our way of seeing ourselves and the world, something we would rather ignore or get rid of. Within that strange and alien something is hid-den an energy and power beyond our wildest dreams. Actually, it has been appearing in our dreams in different guises for years. It has also influenced our lives, flowing like a stream through every house we have ever lived in. It shows up in our creativity, usually unbeknownst to us.

My guess is that the same energy that we use when we create, also creates us. The same power, the same creative spark, the same creative impulse that rises from somewhere deep inside us or from some unknown and unknowable source, also shapes us, creates our dreams, and runs like a golden thread through the tapestry of our lives. Instead of running away from it, like my mother ran from the rumbling, we can embrace it, learn from it, and ask it to guide and help us. Together with that awesome force, we can co-create our lives, our art, and our music.

Try This:

1. Think of a problem you have in your life. State it as a question that you would like answered. You might want to think about questions like, "Who am I? What am I doing here? What is my task in life? How can I make my work, or my relationships, more fulfilling? Where is my place on this earth?" Or you might want to choose something more immediate and not so life shaking. Write the question down on a piece of paper.

2. Think of a difficulty you are having in your creative life. Try to formulate it as a question and write it down as well.

3. Remember your earliest childhood dream. If you remember several, choose the one that was scariest, or the one that repeated itself most often. If you can't remember a dream, think of your very earliest childhood memory. Some people can't remember childhood at all. So try to find the very earliest thing you can remember.

4. Notice what part of that dream or memory you identify with. (For simplicity, let's call it a dream.) It will probably be the part that was "you" in the dream.

5. Notice what part of the dream is most different from you. This may be the part that is threatening to you in the dream. It may be something that scared you, surprised you, or delighted you unexpectedly.

6. Describe that part that is different from you. Be as exact as possible.

7. Become that part that is different from you. Move like it, make sounds like it, feel what it is like to be that. Focus particularly on its energy, not on words it might be saying. Forget the content. Just become that energy. This is your ally.

8. Let your ally energy create. Let it choose a medium and express itself. Do not try to express "yourself" but rather let your ally express *itself*.

9. When you are in the midst of being your ally energy, read your questions about life and creativity. Let the ally energy answer those questions. How would it deal with those problems? Write down the answers.

10. Go back to the ally energy and let that create again. Then ask it how it would live. How would it create your life?

11. Do these answers go along with your normal intentions? If not, have a discussion with that energy. Have it out with your ally until you reach some agreement about how the two of you can co-create your life and your art.

Chapter 15
The Border Song

A raging storm woke me with a start late last night. Lightning blazed. Thunder cracked right on its heels. The night was alive with light and sound. For a few short moments, which seemed to last forever, flashes and roars exploded simultaneously, shaking the fragile panes that separated me from the onslaught. Soon the worst was over. As the storm moved on, my heart slowed to its normal beat. Though grateful to drift back to sleep, I felt a strange longing for the intensity of those crashes.

Loud banging woke me this morning. Still in that state between dreams and this world, I had no idea where I was or what could cause that frightful sound. Then consensus reality took hold and I remembered that my apartment building is being renovated, and I realized that the workers must be hammering on the wall just behind my pillow. My fear was replaced with curiosity. Why two such similar experiences, and why now? What is trying to wake me up? Where am I asleep? What banging and crashing is trying to get my attention?

Yesterday I experienced writer's block. After writing the following short paragraph, I went completely blank:

"This book is filled with my truth. Please take and apply what is useful to your music, your creativity, and your life. Leave the rest behind like an old pair of shoes."

I really liked that paragraph. I felt it was important to not impose my ideas. I wanted to give you, dear reader, the leeway to take what feels right for you and throw away what doesn't. But then my brain stopped. I didn't know what else to say. I sat for hours in front of my computer, trying all the tricks in my process tool kit to no avail. Why would I get so stuck? I went to bed asking for a guiding dream. Could these experiences hold the answer I sought?

The lightning and the thunder, the hammer banging like a wake-up call, would not dispassionately say, "Use this if you want, but if not, don't bother." They would explode and light up the sky. They would shake the foundations of your thinking, crash your beliefs about yourself and about music. Although I still agree with what I wrote yesterday, a new force is running through me now. *It wants to write.* Perhaps it is needed as a balance to yesterday's detachment. Now is the time to walk my talk.

Wake up, it cries to musicians and artists of all kinds! The strange experience you tend to ignore is a teacher knocking at your gate. The mistake you try to practice into oblivion is the kick of a baby in your belly waiting to be born. The unwanted, the rejected, are presents left at your door by anonymous donors. Don't turn them away! Stop thinking they are enemies to be eradicated. Treat them instead as a lover treats the beloved. Hold them to your breast. Meld with them in divine embrace. Allow them to transform you, your music, and your art from the inside.

Wake up, it cries to music teachers! Your student may be a secret maestro just waiting to share her talents, or a sage in disguise, sent to wake you up to your own music. Her rebellious grunts and rolling eyes could be the first signs of an indomitable dragon about to lift into the air and plunge into the sea. Instead of fighting against all that power, grab hold and go for the ride of your life! Lessons will never be the same.

Wake up, it cries to you who long to be musical! The words you utter from morning until night are but lyrics to a brand new song waiting to be discovered. The sighs and groans you think you understand could be the first strains of an unwritten symphony or the far-off cries of an untamed beast. Music and art are not only things to be enjoyed during your free time but are treasures lying just beneath the surface of your daily interactions.

Wake up, it cries to you who think you could never be musical or creative! Take a vacation from your critic and enjoy the fact that you sound different from anyone else. Celebrate your uniqueness! Or, if you think you are ordinary, just wait until you start following those unintentional sounds and listen to how far from ordinary you become! The music and art inside of you is just waiting to be found, golden nuggets hidden among a thousand pebbles in a stream. But the beauty of this stream is that any of those pebbles, when treated with love, turns by magic into gold.

Wake up, it cries to you who think you could never do the things described in this book! Awareness is the only instrument played in this band. Love is the key in which we play. Mistakes are our favorite tunes. If you are curious about the unintentional, you have just passed the audition. Come, play along!

But wait, another voice breaks in. There are things to learn, methods to apply. Surely it can't be as simple as you make it sound.

Of course not, laughs the hammer. So jump out of your warm bed and get to work. Grab a tool and learn to use it. The thunder calls invitingly: Your pillow is soft and cozy but the night outside is wild and exciting. Up! Up!

The storm passes, but the sky is still lit and rumbling. Is it night or day? The line between the two seems blurred. Is this dream or waking reality? Perhaps the difference is not so clear as we normally think.

The border between the worlds is getting hazy. Was this book about music or self-discovery? If you follow these strange ideas, will it affect your playing or your personality? If you incorporate them into your daily practice, will you become even stranger than you already are?

Who is the process worker and who is the musician? Who is the teacher and who is the student? The borders between the roles become fluid, changing constantly with the dreaming process that is inside us, all around us, and connecting us.

That doesn't mean we're all just one undifferentiated mass. Diversity is staggering. Our differences make life rich, fascinating, and exquisitely tasty. Each of us dreams the dreams that are meant only for us, hears the inner music that only we can hear. Each of us moves in our own way across the landscape, co-creating reality as our steps make their imprint on the ground.

As we follow that path that is uniquely ours, a subtle shift happens. The outer diversity that gave birth to our individuality gives way to an inner diversity. We start to discover that everything is inside of us. Our worst enemies show up in our dreams. We hear our most loved friends in our own voices. The conflicts we read about in the newspaper now seem surprisingly similar to what happens at our own kitchen tables. We start to feel as solid as rocks or as fluid as water, as focused as an eagle diving for prey or as detached as a jellyfish floating on the waves. All of humanity, all of Nature, turns up in our double signals. Do we have the courage to follow this moment-to-moment process of discovery? The freedom to live it and let it shape our music and art?

Freedom beckons. The freedom to live, feel, sing, play, and express everything inside us. The freedom to know who's hiding there behind our eyes, and to give her the microphone. When we find our own voice, we can use it in the service of those who have no voice. Free, we can be better allies to those who are not yet free. We will not think of them as clients or students or people needing our help, for we will know that we are they. They are inside of us, struggling to live, to breathe, to sing, to create.

By living our lives with a passion for awareness, we can be

creative in every moment. Music and life become original, vital. Where is the distinction between self-discovery and art, between art and life, when everything we do grabs the very stuff of existence in a creative embrace?

The line between dream and reality . . . is you.

Glossary

Ally. An awesome spirit or energy that plagues us and terrifies us but that can potentially help us and guide us through life. Often represented in a childhood dream as the figure(s) that we fear. An ally can often be discovered by working with chronic or life-threatening illnesses.

Archetype. An archetype is a tendency for an experience to happen again and again. This tendency is cross-cultural and extends throughout time. Archetypes often show themselves in dreams, as well as in mythological motifs that appear worldwide (like the story of the flood). (See *Trickster.*)

Channel. A channel is a mode of perception. It's useful to know in which channel a process is happening. In other words, it is useful to know how we experience the process. If we know this, then it is easier to follow the process in the direction it is already trying to go.

    The main perceptual channels are

Visual channel: seeing

Auditory channel: hearing, includes music, sound, all paralinguistic phenomena

Verbal channel: speech and all linguistic phenomena

Body-feeling channel (also called "proprioception"): includes inner body feelings as well as tactile sensations, feelings of pressure, weight, temperature, etc.

Movement channel (also known as kinesthesia): Although we can feel our movements and also see them, the sense of moving is qualitatively different than the sense of feeling without moving, so this is considered a separate channel. The composite channels are:

Relationship channel: Although all the other channels are active when we are in a relationship, something else altogether is actually at play when we relate to another person. As a result, Mindell calls relationship a different channel.

World channel: Again, there is a new quality when we are interacting with the world, or with groups, that is different than what happens in the other channels.

Childhood dream. Some nighttime dreams that occur during our childhoods repeat themselves often. Others only come once. Childhood dreams show, in symbolic form, the life-long patterns that make up a person's life myth. If a person does not remember a childhood dream, it is possible to get the same information by working with the very earliest childhood memory.

Deep democracy. Deep democracy is an idea about the world that all people, and all points of view, need to be represented and given a chance to express themselves, in order for us to make decisions that affect all of us. Deep democracy can also happen internally. This would mean that we should consult all our different parts, and let them all express themselves, when we are making decisions (for instance, a decision about how to play music).

Double signal. A double signal is a signal that does not go along with the rest of what you are trying to sing, play, paint, write, do, etc. It may be a sound, movement, word, etc, that does not go along with the rest of what you are doing. You want to communicate one thing, and another part of you wants to express something else.

Edge. The edge is the border of our identity, the border of who we are, of what we like, of what we can do, of what we know. We can say "she *got to an edge*" when a person reached that border and could go no further, when she was doing something (like starting to play music in a new way) but then stopped, when some inner or outer pressure prevented her from continuing. An edge is supported by a *belief system*, and by *edge figures*. For instance, someone may have an edge to be loud because she believes that it is not nice, and that people should be quiet and gentle. This belief system is supported by edge figures, like her mother who told her to be quiet and nice, or her religion, which tells her that people should be loving and gentle. This belief system and these edge figures make it difficult for the person to "*go over the edge*," or explore behaviors (and music) that are new and different.

Life Myth. Your life myth is the central dynamic in your life, the long-term mythical patterns that structure who you are. Although the dynamic usually stays the same, your relationship to your life myth can change as you live your life and become more aware of your wholeness. Parts of your myth that used to scare or repulse you may become more attractive and helpful as you grow and change.

Metaskill. Metaskills are the feeling attitudes that we use when we apply a skill. For instance, when we learn a new language, we are able to ask how much something costs in a foreign country. This is a skill. We can then speak those words kindly, or shout them impatiently. Our metaskills, the feeling with which we apply our skill, will have a great effect on the response we receive to our question. The same is true when applying any skill, and is especially true when we work with our own (or someone else's) unintentional music. (See chapter 3.)

Occupied and unoccupied channels. When something happens in a channel that is close to our identity, intention, and awareness, we say that channel is occupied. When something happens in a channel that someone or something else did (we did not do it), that goes against our intention, or is far from our awareness, then we call that channel unoccupied. As with primary and secondary processes, there is a continuum between more occupied and less occupied. It is not either/or.

Primary process. The primary process is our momentary sense of ourselves. If we intend to do something, this is primary. If we identify with a certain trait, this trait is primary. If we are aware of something, it is primary. If we do something (as opposed to it happening to us) it is more primary. Processes are on a continuum between primary and secondary. They are not black and white, either/or. Something is more or less primary than something else. The primary process is sometimes unconscious. This means that I may not realize that I think of myself in a certain way. I may, for instance, go around feeling weak. But if you were to tell me that I am weak, I may say it is not true. On the other hand, if you would tell me I am strong, I would feel this is even less true. So weakness would be more primary, and strength would be more secondary on the continuum. Primary and secondary processes are momentary descriptions. In the next moment, what was secondary might become primary, and vice versa.

Process. The simplest definition of process is that something happens, then it stops, and then something else happens. Things (and people) continually change and transform. Process is a term describing that ever-changing flow.

Secondary process. The secondary process is what we think of as "not-me." If something unintentional happens to me, this is secondary. If I do not identify with it, that is secondary. If I am less aware of something, it is secondary. If someone else does something, rather than me doing it, it is secondary. Again, there is a continuum between *more primary* and *more secondary*, rather than an either/or split.

Signal. A signal is the smallest manifestation of process. Whenever we perceive something happening, we perceive a signal (or a series of signals). Any sound or movement or word or feeling (etc.) that you notice is a signal. A signal can also be thought of as a communication. It is a bit of a message being sent from one person to another, or from one part of you to another part of you, or from the world to you.

Subchannel. Subchannels give us a way to differentiate between the various aspects of a certain channel. Auditory subchannels are the basic components of music and sound. Thinking of sound and music in these terms helps us to be more neutral, noninterpretive, and precise when we describe what we hear. (See chapter 7.)

The main auditory subchannels are:
Volume: the loudness or quietness of a sound or note.

Pitch: the highness or lowness of a sound or note. (When a police siren goes up and down, it is the pitch that changes. The keys on the right side of a piano keyboard have a higher pitch than those on the left.)

Timbre: the quality of a sound that distinguishes it from other sounds of the same pitch and volume. (Imagine Luciano Pavarotti and Louis Armstrong singing the same song. For a more direct experience, start speaking aloud and then hold your nose while you continue speaking. The change you hear is a change in timbre.)

Time: includes how fast or slow the music or sound is (tempo), and the differences in duration of particular sounds or notes (rhythm). (If you play a song on a tape player, and then speed up the tape, the rhythm of the music stays the same but the tempo gets faster. If, though, you play a blues and a waltz at the same tempo or speed—each beat takes one second, for instance—the rhythms of the two kinds of music are still different.)

These subchannels can be combined. In this way, practically all music can be described by using just the four terms defined above.

Melody can be described as a succession of different pitches over time.

Harmony/discord can be described as consisting of two or more notes when played or sung at the same time.

Dynamic can be described as the relationship of different volumes over time.

Tao. The Tao is impossible to define. The closest I can come is to say that it is a dynamic order that structures the way things are. It can be thought of as the order of Nature. It is the deeper pattern behind what we normally perceive. Taoism is an ancient Chinese philosophy and way of life that has been most eloquently expressed by sages like Lao Tsu and Chuang Tsu. The Taoists' ideal is to follow the Tao; this means noticing and aligning themselves with "what is." Taoists try to do nothing that goes against the Tao, and to only do things that go along with (or support) Nature and the natural course of things. The Tao is in a process of constant flux and change. Perhaps it is better to say that the Tao is itself a process of constant flux and change. Taoists try to flow and change along with it.

Trickster. The trickster is an archetypal motif, personified by the Greek god Hermes, the Norse god Loki, the Native American Trickster or Coyote, etc. The trickster is a culture breaker and culture maker, who goes against the norms of society to create new things and new ways of being. The trickster makes jokes and plays tricks on people and gods. In some traditions, he learns through unconsciousness; by doing things unconsciously, he discovers himself and creates the world.

Unintentional. "Unintentional" is, simply, a word that describes those things that are not intended. But I am using it here in a wider sense. I sometimes even use it as a noun ("the unintentional") to include anything we are not aware of, that does not go along with our plans or our intentions, and that is outside our identity. This is what process work calls a secondary process. But secondary process sounds so technical. I like "unintentional," because it carries with it (for me, at least) an intimation of the unknown, of something happening to us that is out of our control, of the mystery.

Bibliography

Ausebel, N. *A Treasury of Jewish Folklore*. New York: Crown Publishers, Inc., 1948.

Basho. *On Love and Barley*. Translated by L. Stryk. Harmondsworth, Middlesex: Penguin Classics, 1985.

Blofeld, J. *Taoism: The Road to Immortality*. Boston: Shambhala, 1985.

Bloomberg, M. "Introduction: Approaches to Creativity." In *Creativity: Theory and Research*. New Haven: College and University Press, 1973.

Brown, N.O. *Hermes the Thief*. New York: Vintage Books, 1947.

Cage, J. *Silence*. Middletown, CT: Wesleyan University Press, 1961.

Cleveland, J. *Somebody's Knocking, Part II*. Savgos Music, Inc./BMI, James Cleveland Music/MBI, 1990.

Coleridge, S.T. *Selected Poetry*. Edited by H.J. Jackson. Oxford University Press, 1997.

Cook, N. *A Guide to Musical Analysis*. New York: George Braziller, 1987.

Diamond, J. *Patterns of Communication: Towards a Natural Science of Behavior*, 1988.

Eliade, M. (1964). *Shamanism: Archaic Techniques of Ecstasy*. Translated by W.R. Trask. Princeton: Princeton University Press, 1964.

Freud, S. "The Relation of the Poet to Day-Dreaming." In Vol. 4, *Collected Papers*, translated by J. Riviere, 173-183. London: Hogarth, 1934. Originally published in 1908.

Freud, S. "Formulations Regarding the Two Principles in Mental Functioning." In Vol. 4, *Collected Papers*, 13-21. London: Hogarth, 1934. Originally published in 1911.

Freud, S. "Dostoyevski and Parricide." In Vol. 5, *Collected Papers*, translated by J. Riviere, 222-242). London: Hogarth. Originally published in1928.

Goodbread, J. H. *The Dreambody Toolkit*. New York: Routledge & Kegan Paul, 1987.

Goodbread, J. *Radical Intercourse: How Dreams Unite Us in Love, Conflict and Other Inevitable Relationships*. Portland, OR: Lao Tse Press, 1997.

Herrigel, E. *Zen in the Art of Archery*. Translated by R.F.C. Hull. London: Penguin Arkana, 1953.

Homer. *The Homeric Hymns*. Translated by A.N. Athanassakis. Baltimore: The Johns Hopkins University Press, 1976.

Iamblichus. *Iamblichus' Life of Pythagoras*. Translated by T. Taylor. Rochester, VT: Inner Traditions International, 1986.

Jolocho, M and Owczarek, M. Roza w diamancie. In *Remedium* No. 5 (1996): 39.

Jung, C. G. "A Review of the Complex Theory." In *The Collected Works of C. G. Jung*. 2d ed. Vol. 8. Edited by G. Adler et al., and translated by C. Hull, 92-104. Princeton: Princeton University Press, 1960. Originally published in 1948.

Jung, C. G. "On the Nature of Dreams." In *The Collected Works of C. G. Jung*. 2d ed. Vol. 8. Edited by G. Adler et al., and translated by C. Hull, 281-297. Princeton: Princeton University Press, 1960. Originally published in 1948.

Jung, C. G. "The Structure of the Psyche." In *The Collected Works of C. G. Jung.* 2d ed. Vol. 8. Edited by G. Adler et al., and translated by C. Hull, 139-158. Princeton: Princeton University Press, 1960. Originally published in 1931.

Jung, C. G. "The Tavistock Lectures." In *The Collected Works of C. G. Jung.* 2d ed. Vol. 18. Edited by G. Adler et al., and translated by C. Hull, 5-182. Princeton: Princeton University Press, 1969.

Jung, C. G. "The Function of the Unconscious." In *The Collected Works of C. G. Jung.* 2d ed. Vol. 7. Edited by G. Adler et al., and translated by C. Hull, 173-187. Princeton: Princeton University Press, 1966. Originally published in 1935.

Kaplan, A. S. *The Hidden Dance: An Introduction to Process-Oriented Movement Work.* Master's thesis, Antioch University, 1986.

Kerenyi, K. (1976). *Hermes: Guide of Souls.* Translated by M. Stein. Dallas, TX: Spring, 1976. Originally published in 1944.

Lao Tse Press. (1994/1995). *Journal of Process Oriented Psychology: Creativity and Arts in Process Work, Spirituality and Life,* 6 (1994/1995): 2.

Mindell, A. *Dreambody: The Body's Role in Revealing the Self.* Boston: Sigo Press, 1982.

Mindell, A. *River's Way.* London: Routledge & Kegan Paul, 1985.

Mindell, A. *Working with the Dreaming Body.* London: Routledge & Kegan Paul, 1985.

Mindell, A. *The Dreambody in Relationships.* London: Routledge & Kegan Paul, 1987.

Mindell, A. *City Shadows: Psychological Interventions in Psychiatry.* London: Routledge & Kegan Paul, 1988.

Mindell, A. *Coma: Key to Awakening.* Boston: Shambhala, 1989.

Mindell, A. *The Year I: Global Process Work.* London: Arkana, 1989.

Mindell, A. *Working on Yourself Alone: Inner Dreambody Work.* London: Arkana, 1990.

Mindell, A. *The Leader as Martial Artist*. San Francisco: Harper San Francisco, 1992.

Mindell, A. *The Shaman's Body*. San Francisco: Harper San Francisco, 1993.

Mindell, A. *Sitting in the Fire*. Portland, OR. Lao Tse Press, 1995.

Mindell, A. K. "Magic: Notes on Some of the Magical Elements of Process Work." *The Journal of Process Oriented Psychology*, 2, 1 (1989): 17-31.

Mindell, A. K. *Metaskills: The Spiritual Art of Therapy*. Tempe, AZ: New Falcon Publications, 1995.

Minuchin, S., Rosman, B. L., and Baker, L. S. *Psychosomatic Families: Anorexia Nervosa in Context*. Cambridge, MA: Harvard University Press, 1978.

Mitchell, C. *Celestial Navigation*, 1998.

Moyne, J. and Barks, C. *Open Secret: Versions of Rumi*. Putney, VT: Threshold Books, 1984.

Moyne, J. and Barks, C. *Unseen Rain: Quatrains of Rumi*. Putney, VT: Threshold Books, 1986.

Nietzsche, F. "The Birth of Tragedy." In *The Birth of Tragedy and the Case of Wagner*. Translated by W. Kaufmann, 15-144. New York: Vintage Books, 1967. Originally published in 1886.

Prothero, S. Introduction to *Big Sky Mind: Buddhism & the Beat Generation* by C. Tonkinson. New York: Riverhead Books, 1995.

Radin, P. *The Trickster: A Study in American Indian Mythology*. New York: Shocken Books, 1956.

Reps, P., ed. *Zen Flesh, Zen Bones*. Harmondsworth, Middlesex, England: Penguin Books, 1957.

Rilke, R.M. *Letters to a Young Poet*. Translated by Stephen Mitchell. Boston: Shambhala, 1993.

Ronan, C.A. and Needham, J. *The New Science & Civilization in China: 1*. Cambridge: Cambridge University Press, 1978.

Straub, S. *Stalking Your Inner Critic*. Ph.D. diss., The Union Institute, 1990.

The Jewish Publication Society of America, trans. *The Holy Scriptures*. Philadelphia: The Jewish Publication Society of America, 1955.

Tsu, Lao. *Tao Te Ching*. Translated by S. Mitchell. New York: Harper Perennial, 1988.

Van Over, R., ed. *Taoist Tales*. New York: Mentor Books, 1973.

Watts, A. *Tao: The Watercourse Way*. Harmondsworth, Middlesex, England: Penguin Books, 1975.

Wieger, L. and Bryce, D., trans. *Wisdom of the Daoist Masters*. Llanerch, Felinfach, Lampeter, Dyfed, Wales: Llanerch Enterprises, 1984.

Wilhelm, R. and Baynes, C.F., trans. *The I Ching* or *Book of Changes*. 3d ed. Princeton: Princeton University Press, 1967. Originally published in 1956.

Yeats, W.B. "The Symbolism of Poetry." In *Essays*, 188-202. New York: The MacMillan Company, 1924.

About the Author

Lane Arye, Ph.D., is an internationally known process-oriented therapist and teacher. He developed "Unintentional Music"—a way of using process work with professional and amateur musicians as they play or sing to help them transform both their music and themselves. He teaches unintentional music, creativity, process work, and conflict resolution throughout the United States and worldwide.

Arye is himself a singer and songwriter who has performed in clubs, concerts, and festivals in the United States and Europe. He maintains a residence and private practice in the San Francisco Bay area of California.

You may contact the author by e-mail at lane@processworklane.com or visit his website at: www.processworklane.com

Hampton Roads Publishing Company

. . . for the evolving human spirit

Hampton Roads Publishing Company
publishes books on a variety of subjects,
including metaphysics, health, integrative medicine,
visionary fiction, and other related topics.

For a copy of our latest catalog, call toll-free
(800) 766-8009, or send your name and address to:

Hampton Roads Publishing Company, Inc.
1125 Stoney Ridge Road
Charlottesville, VA 22902

e-mail: hrpc@hrpub.com
www.hrpub.com